THE UPSTART GUIDE TO

OWNING AND MANAGING
A BAR OR TAVERN

THE UPSTART GUIDE TO
Owning and Managing a Bar or Tavern

Roy S. Alonzo

UPSTART PUBLISHING COMPANY, INC.

Published by Upstart Publishing Company, Inc.
a division of Dearborn Publishing Group, Inc.
155 North Wacker Drive
Chicago, Illinois 60606-1719
(800)235-8866 or (312)836-4400

Neither the author nor the publisher of this book is engaged in rendering, by the sale of
this book, legal, accounting, or other professional services. The reader is encouraged to
employ the services of a competent professional in such matters.

Library of Congress Cataloging-in-Publication Data
Alonzo, Roy S.
    The upstart guide to owning and managing a bar or tavern / Roy S. Alonzo.
        p. cm.
    Includes index.
    ISBN 0-936894-67-9
    1. Bars (Drinking establishments)—Management. 2. Taverns (Inns)—
Management. I. Title.
TX95.7.A49 1995
647.95'068—dc20   94-26954
                                                                           CIP

Cover design by Paul Perlow Design, New York, NY.

Printed in the United States of America
10 9 8 7

For a complete catalog of Upstart's small business publications, call (800) 235-8866.

I sincerely thank my wife,

DARLENE

to whom I dedicate this book,
for her cheerful encouragement

CONTENTS

PREFACE

Remember the last time you were in a bar, having a great time—enjoying good drinks and food with convivial friends? Did the thought cross your mind that it was a wonderful bar and you admiringly wished it were yours? If you have an entrepreneurial bent, that would not have been an uncommon thought. Most of us are attracted by the places we like, especially if they appear to be highly profitable.

The purpose of this book is to give readers a sense of what the bar business is like, to make them aware of what is required to enter it, and to help them evaluate whether it is the right business for them. It is intended to acquaint readers with a logical course of action for starting a bar, should they decide to enter the business, and to give them insights and techniques for operating a bar. The contents of this book are presented as a source of ideas, methods, and procedures as well as a resource on where to go for specific information.

Prior to the Prohibition era, the food and beverage industry had very few management controls. Liquor profits were sufficiently high as to disinterest proprietors from expending a great deal of time or effort on controls. Management was conducted to a large extent by whim and personality, rather than by systems and procedures. When the Prohibition Act was implemented in 1920 many proprietors panicked at the thought of having to survive with only food sales.

The large companies took action to protect their investment. They engaged accountants to study their operations and recommend ways to operate their food businesses profitably. The accountants compared the food service industry to other industries and concluded it had many similarities. Other industries have three basic spheres of activity: 1) procurement and warehousing, 2) manufacturing, and 3) sales and service. The food and beverage industry has the same three, called by different names: food and beverage purchasing, food and beverage production (bartending), and sales and table service.

When viewed that way, it became obvious that the same kinds of accountability and controls used by industry in general could be adapted to the food service industry. That was done, and the industry not only survived, it profited. After the Prohibition Act was repealed in 1933, legalizing the sale of liquor, the question arose, "Do we go back to the old ways, or continue to use accounting controls?" The answer was clearly to continue with controls on food operations and to expand them to the liquor side of the business as well. That was the birth of beverage controls, as we know them today.

Hotel companies, restaurant chains, the National Restaurant Association, and institutions of higher education that offer hospitality programs have been the most active in developing management systems and control procedures. However, even with a developed state of the art, many independent beverage operations still function with inadequate controls, a shortcoming this book will address.

For many years, the term *guests* has been used in reference to persons who patronize hospitality establishments. This is done to underscore the fact that they are welcome in our houses of business. However, in spite of the good intentions behind the term, it is used all too blithely. Most of us have had the occasion of reading slogans like "we value our guests" only to experience poor service and an inferior meal—and no one seeming to care. What is worse is that this is not a rare occurrence. Therefore, the term *customers* is used in this book. It is intended to be a reminder that customers are people who favor us with their patronage. We owe them the best product and service we can provide. The notion that we value our patrons should not have to be spoken or printed, it should be demonstrated in ways our customers will appreciate.

Laws vary from state to state and between the various levels of government. Where any laws are discussed in this book, it is only to make the reader aware of their existence. Consequently, nothing in this book is offered as legal advice or an interpretation of a law and should not be construed as such. Information of that kind should be obtained from attorneys and the appropriate government officials, as should advice on accounting matters be sought from specialized professionals.

The mention of any product names in this book is done merely for illustrative purposes and should not be deemed an endorsement. Likewise, where products are mentioned, the omission of any particular products is not in any way a reflection on such products.

Finally, this book is intended to stimulate thinking about the bar and tavern business, answer a variety of questions and present an assortment of management tools that may be used to operate a bar or tavern. To those who may someday become proprietors of a beverage hospitality establishment, we wish you a full measure of success and happiness in your quest to achieve your goals.

ACKNOWLEDGMENTS

The contributions of many people and companies helped make this book possible. I would like to thank the Perlick Corporation and in particular Thomas E. McGee, Sales Promotion Manager, for information, photos, and drawings; Rusty Hammer and Bill MacMillan for sharing their business experiences; Peter Egelston and Paul Murphy of the Portsmouth Brewery and Smuttynose Brewing Company for information on micro breweries; Anheuser-Busch Inc. of St. Louis, MO, for information on handling beer and brewing; the Massachusetts Liquor Commission for information on the liquor laws of that state; the New Hampshire Liquor Commission for information on the liquor laws of that state; the Distilled Spirits Council of the United States for helpful statistical information; and the National Licensed Beverage Association of West Alexandria, VA, and M. Shanken Communications, Inc., of New York, NY, for useful information on the alcoholic beverage industry.

For the use of photos, I would like to thank Bud Young, photographer; the New England Center of Durham, NH; and Schramsberg Vineyards and Cellars of Calistoga, CA. Beyond the above, I would also like to thank Becky for her secretarial help.

THE BAR BUSINESS

In colonial times a tavern was considered a place that "provided food, drink and lodging for man and his beast." Today, a generally accepted definition of a tavern is an establishment where alcoholic beverages are sold to be drunk on the premises.

Most bars are associated with food operations, as in the case of restaurants, and some offer limited food menus of their own, giving rise to the question—Is the establishment a restaurant that sells liquor or a bar that sells food? To that, there is no universal answer. An establishment's identification in the public's view is largely a function of how its management chooses to position it in the marketplace and what its greatest source of revenue is—food or alcoholic beverages.

Many bars are linked with entertainment or other activities. The term "bar" is commonly used today in reference to many businesses that sell alcoholic beverages—taverns and pubs, restaurant bars, country club lounges, nightclub bars, airport lounges, bowling alley bars, hotel tap rooms, and ballroom bars, to name but a few.

A Long History

Alcoholic beverages have deep roots in American history. Licenses were held by many honorable men, pillars of the church, leaders of the community, and political and military figures. Taverns were often the secret meeting places of such prominent patriots as Washington, Franklin,

Figure 1.1: Acorns in the Woods, a comfortable lounge in the New England Center in Durham, NH. (Photo by Bud Young.)

Jefferson, Revere, and the Adams brothers, during the early revolutionary days. After the Revolutionary War, George Washington distilled whiskey and Sam Adams was a brewer. Abraham Lincoln held a tavern license in Springfield, Illinois.

For the person seeking an attractive return on investment, the retail beverage business can offer opportunities and challenges. It must, however, be run in a businesslike manner and utilize the same management practices and controls required for any successful business. Beyond that, the owner of a bar or tavern must have a keen sense of market savvy. Knowledge of one's customers' wants and needs is critical to success.

So You Want to be in the Bar Business

Some people frequent bars to socialize, others to relax or watch a sporting event, and still others to transact business affairs. Whatever the occasion, most people have enjoyable memories of their experiences in bars. So much so, that some decide to enter the beverage business for a livelihood.

There is a great attraction to the bar business. The chance to meet interesting people, to work in a social atmosphere, and to be with people having fun. These are strong attractions, but should not be principal reasons for entering the business.

Not for Everyone

Not everyone who likes to eat out should be in the restaurant business. The same applies to bars. Bars have excellent profit-making potential when they are properly run, but they also require long hours, painstaking attention to details, working on weekends and holidays, and sometimes putting up with nuisance customers. These are the realities of the business, and you cannot expect to have a successful operation without being willing to endure these hardships.

Increasingly, we find other professional and commercial people—pilots, police, firemen, doctors and nurses, as well as people in the retailing and service fields—also working odd hours, weekends, and holidays. The redeeming feature of the bar business is it offers the opportunity for substantial profits.

The bar business is one that people like or dislike, and those who like it seem to love it—even with its unusual characteristics. A well-managed, ethically run beverage business can offer a high degree of job satisfaction. It can also render prestige to its owners in the form of social acceptance and public recognition.

The Rusty Hammer

If you don't get there early, you'll have to wait in line. Such is the case, on many days at the Rusty Hammer in Portsmouth, New Hampshire. The Rusty Hammer, named after one of its owners, Rusty Hammer, is a 200-seat bar and restaurant located midway between Portsmouth's downtown shopping center and its beautiful waterfront park.

The small New England seaport town has a population of about 20,000, which doubles in the summer with an influx of tourists and vacationers. It is strategically located between a string of popular beaches to the south and famous brand discount malls to the north and west. During the boom years of the early '80s, the city was reputed to have more restaurants per capita than any other in New England. Over the years many restaurants have come and gone in Portsmouth, but the Rusty Hammer, a success from its first day continues to thrive. The reason why?—the owners know the market. They know what their customers want, and they work hard to give it to them.

A native and lifelong resident of Portsmouth, Rusty Hammer left college in the early '70s to became a bartender at a local restaurant. After three years he tried a stint at selling investments and insurance. "It didn't take long," he says, "to find out that was not my cup of tea." Whereupon he and a friend, Bill MacMillan decided to join forces and go into the bar and restaurant business.

They decided to buy a small, obscure, restaurant that was for sale for $14,000. Rusty and Bill each borrowed $12,000 from their parents, enough to buy the business and have $10,000 of working capital.

They applied for a liquor license from the state, and food and health permits from the city. Most of the existing equipment in the restaurant was very old, and they also acquired used equipment from other restaurants.

Family members and friends with trade skills helped with the renovations. Rusty remembers how they were so busy running around, making do on a shoestring budget, that it was not until two weeks before their scheduled opening date that someone asked, "What are we going to have on the menu?"

"The hardest part was the kitchen," he explained. "Equipping the kitchen, planning the menu, and developing a food production system were the most difficult tasks. The bar was not a problem."

The original Rusty Hammer had 65 seats when it opened, and the menu was basic. Asked about his funniest memory of their start-up, Rusty recalled, "The day we opened, a lady ordered a Reuben sandwich, and the cook didn't know if it took roast beef or corned beef."

Through the years they learned fast, and they learned well. Their priority was always to stay with the basics their clientele wanted—good food and drinks at reasonable prices, served in a pleasant setting. Today, the Rusty Hammer occupies an entire corner block. Its clientele ranges from blue collar workers to professionals, from people in their 20s to people in their 60s and 70s.

The Rusty Hammer serves breakfast, lunch, and dinner. On weekend mornings people wait in line to eat in the upstairs dining room, where the sun streams through the stained glass panels. The food is tasty and piled

Figure 1.2: The Rusty Hammer, located near Portsmouth's historic colonial village, Strawbery Banke, is a popular site for both tourists and local residents. (Photo supplied by Rusty Hammer.)

high, which is what their customers want. Their dinner menu includes steaks, chicken, fish, and the house specialty—gourmet burgers. Menu prices range from a modest $3.95 to $8.95. In the evening, its bar is usually filled with people enjoying a mellow atmosphere that allows conversation.

The bar at the Rusty Hammer has experienced a lot of societal changes in attitudes toward alcohol. The legal drinking age has gone up from 18 to 21, and the legal level of intoxication down from .10 to .08 blood alcohol. The bar has cut down on the number of 100% proof products, in favor of lower alcohol products in the 80% to 90% proof range. Sales of nonalcoholic beers are steadily increasing each year.

Wine sales are steady, and beer is still the best selling beverage at the bar. The Rusty Hammer carries a broad variety of bottled beers and ales and three draft beers on tap, including micro-brewed Sam Adams. One of the newest summer drinks at the Rusty Hammer bar is called a Frozen Jello, made with raspberry jello, vodka, and raspberry schnapps topped with whipped cream and served in a paper cup.

Continuity means a lot at the Rusty Hammer. The menu still has the old favorites that made the bar popular, and the management's philosophy continues to be "serve the kind of food and drinks that people want, at reasonable prices." The owners take great pride in the mainstay on their original menu, the burger. Rusty exclaims, "There will always be a great burger on their menu." Not only does the burger dates back to the beginning of the business, one of the original cooks is still there. Also, Jimmy the bartender has been with the Rusty Hammer for 12 years.

Over the years, the partners, whose skills complement each other, have worked out a one-week-on and one-week-off schedule for themselves. Realizing that an eating and drinking establishment requires constant oversight, they work whatever hours are required when on schedule— some days six hours, other days ten. The system of alternating weeks allows a reasonable amount of time off and yet assures constant supervision of the establishment.

The Rusty Hammer is a well-regarded bar and restaurant that exemplifies the entrepreneurial possibilities in the food and beverage business. When asked what advice he would give to a person who is thinking about entering the business, Rusty Hammer responded, "You have to stay on top of the changes that are always going on—recognize the shifts in dining preferences and spending habits—and be able to flow with the changes."

A Typical Day in a Manager's Life

An owner/manager of a bar can wear many hats in the course of a day. How many will depend on his or her particular skills and interests and the size of the establishment. In a large operation, many duties are to be delegated to office managers and other staff people, but in a small, start-up businesses, monetary constraints usually require owners to do many things themselves.

A typical day could include: checking the previous days receipts and preparing the bank deposit, inventorying the bar and ordering stock, preparing work schedules, working on the payroll, talking to salespeople, interviewing applicants for jobs, placing advertisements with media representatives, conducting meetings with employees, repairing a broken piece of equipment, checking out food and drink prices, planning new menu items, working up sales promotion ideas, checking on the quality of products and customer service, and working the floor to meet and greet the clientele.

Few jobs present such a broad variety of challenges and allow a person to exercise so great a range of skills. One thing is certain in the bar business—it is never boring.

Can Someone Else Manage For You?

Yes, provided the person is knowledgeable about the liquor business, honest, dedicated, and willing to make the same kind of personal sacrifices that you would be willing to make. The degree to which such a person may succeed will depend largely upon the motivation and system of rewards you give.

Is Bar Ownership For You?

The bar business is an entrepreneurial experience and as such has risks, disappointments, seemingly endless demands for time and money, and no sure-fire guarantee of success. Some people thrive on challenges, which bring out their best qualities. Others feel insecure and uncomfortable when faced with uncertainty. Are you cut out to be an entrepreneur? Are you willing to risk your savings for a business? Are you amenable to a second mortgage on your house and borrowing from friends and relatives?

Are you willing and able to work 12 hours or more a day, 7 days a week, if necessary? Can you tolerate the uncertainty that might prevail during the infant years of the business? Can you stand the pressure of being the leader and shouldering the responsibility of keeping a business afloat when all others may have given up? Are you willing to forgo your social life and very likely your vacation during the start-up period, which may be protracted?

The answers to these questions are an indication of your passion for small business. Most people prefer the stability of a 9 to 5 job with a steady paycheck, and there is absolutely nothing wrong with that. But, if you are the type of person who thrives on seeing your creation grow, in spite of the sacrifices required, then being in business for yourself may be an exhilarating and profitable experience for you.

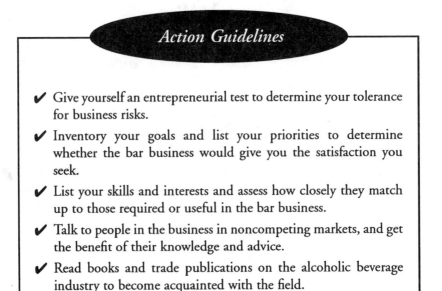

Action Guidelines

- ✔ Give yourself an entrepreneurial test to determine your tolerance for business risks.
- ✔ Inventory your goals and list your priorities to determine whether the bar business would give you the satisfaction you seek.
- ✔ List your skills and interests and assess how closely they match up to those required or useful in the bar business.
- ✔ Talk to people in the business in noncompeting markets, and get the benefit of their knowledge and advice.
- ✔ Read books and trade publications on the alcoholic beverage industry to become acquainted with the field.

START-UP REQUIREMENTS

So, you have considered the issues discussed in Chapter 1 and have decided the bar business may be for you. The next step is to determine what is required to open a bar.

Financial Requirements

The amount of money required to start a bar will depend on the size of the project you have in mind. You can obtain cost estimates on a per seat or a square footage basis from a book entitled *Means' Building Construction Cost Data* (R. S. Means Co., Kingston, MA) a copy of which should be available at your local library. You will need finances for three stages of your project.

1. *Initial Planning:* accounting and legal resources, market research, and general expenses such as telephone, duplicating, transportation, etc.

2. *Construction and Acquisition of Equipment:* building or renovating the facility, purchasing and installing the necessary equipment, obtaining the appropriate operating supplies.

3. *Pre-Opening Expenses and Working Capital:* Cleaning up after construction, advertising, hiring and training a staff, and having adequate funds to meet payroll and pay other bills until your cash flow builds to where it can sustain current operational costs.

Sources of Financing

To a great degree, you must depend upon your own resources, partners, or investors. Most financial institutions won't lend money for new food or beverage operations unless the borrower has adequate collateral to make the loan virtually risk free. This is due to current tight banking policies and the historically high failure rate in the industry.

Following is a list of sources of funds, including some often overlooked.

- Personal savings
- Taking in partners
- Incorporating
- Cash value of life insurance policies
- Loans from relatives
- Loans from friends
- Collateralized bank loans
- Credit terms from equipment suppliers
- Credit from food suppliers
- Finance companies
- Small Business Administration loans

Personal Requirements

The personal skills required of an owner of a bar are largely determined by how active he or she wishes to become. Bartending skills are useful when an employee does not show up on time and during unexpected rush periods. Basic accounting skills are also helpful, both for understanding the books and for filling in when the bookkeeper is on vacation.

What it comes down to is an owner can pay other people to do the tasks that need to be performed, or the owner may personally do some things. The motivation for owner involvement is usually to save money or to keep a tighter control on operations.

In addition to skill requirements, there are attitude requirements. An owner of a bar should truly enjoy serving the public. Satisfying the clientele should be the uppermost priority of a bar. Owners must be persistent in their training and supervision to communicate this message to all employees.

Location Requirements

A bar must be accessible to its target market. If it caters to business people at noontime, it must be within a few minutes of their workplace. If its customers arrive by car, it must have a nearby and safe parking area. If it wishes to attract tourists, it should be near tourist attractions. Choosing a good location is perhaps the most important task in the entire process of starting a bar. Site selection is discussed in detail in Chapter 3.

Legal Requirements

Aside from money and a good location, there are important legal requirements. The liquor business is tightly regulated. Without all of the necessary licenses, permits, and approvals you cannot open for business.

There are three levels of control for bars and taverns—federal, state, and local (city, town, and county). Federal laws apply uniformly in all 50 states and the District of Columbia, but state and local laws vary from one jurisdiction to another.

You should consult with the appropriate officials at all three levels of government early in the planning phase of your project, to determine the specific requirements that apply to your situation. The appendices of this book contain resource lists of licensing commissions and other agencies that can advise you.

Federal Requirements and Controls

The federal control agencies are the Bureau of Alcohol, Tax and Firearms (BATF), the Department of Labor, and the Internal Revenue Service. Their main concerns are

- the regulation of manufacture, transportation, import, and export of alcoholic beverages;

- the adherence to federal labor laws; and
- the collection of taxes.

Special Occupational Tax Stamp

The BATF, a division of the Treasury Department, issues a *Special Occupational Tax* stamp. Without that stamp, a proposed liquor establishment cannot legally open for business. The Special Tax Stamp is a receipt for payment of the Special Occupational Tax. It is not a federal license and does not confer any privileges on the dealer.

The law defines a retail dealer as "a person who sells alcoholic beverages to any person other than a dealer." This includes all establishments that sell alcoholic beverages for on-premise consumption, such as bars and restaurants. The Special Occupational Tax must be paid each year, on or before July 1.

To pay the tax you must obtain and file a Special Tax Registration and Return, Alcohol and Tobacco form ATF F 5630.5 (10/93). After your initial payment of this tax, you should receive a "renewal registration and return" each year prior to the due date.

The Special Tax Stamp covers only one place of business. If business is conducted at more than one location, a separate Special Tax stamp must be obtained for each location. Persons engaged in the sale of wine, beer, or distilled spirits who willfully fail to pay the tax become liable to a fine of not more than $5,000, imprisonment for not more than two years, or both.

Any changes in location or ownership must be reported to the BATF within 30 days of their occurrence. Inspections by a BATF agent will occur periodically, therefore the Special Tax Stamp should be prominently posted or kept readily available. If your Special Tax Stamp is lost or destroyed, you should contact the BATF immediately to obtain a *Certificate in Lieu of Lost or Destroyed Special Tax Stamp.*

Records of Purchases

Another requirement of the BATF is that every retail dealer must either keep a record in book form showing the date and quantity of all distilled spirits, wine, and beer received on his premises and from whom received or keep all invoices of, and bills for, all distilled spirits, wine, and beer received.

It is also required that all distilled spirits bottles in a licensed beverage establishment must have anti-tampering closures on them, of the type that when broken leave a portion of the closure on the bottle. Prior to 1985, Internal Revenue strip stamps were glued to the cap and neck of the bottles.

It is a punishable violation for a retail dealer to reuse or refill liquor bottles with distilled spirits or any substance, including water. Violations are punishable by fines of not more than $1,000, imprisonment for not more than one year, or both.

For complete details on the federal liquor laws and regulations, call your nearest BATF office and ask for free booklet ATF P 5170.2 (8/89).

Another growth agency is the Department of Labor, which administers the provisions of the *Fair Labor Standards Act.* Its main concerns are with conformance to the federal minimum wage laws and discriminatory practices. Most employers' dealings on labor issues are conducted with state labor departments. In the event state and federal laws vary, as sometimes happens with minimum wage levels, the higher of the two minimum wage rates prevails.

The Internal Revenue Service requires a retail dealer of alcoholic beverages to obtain an Employer Identification Number. This is done by filing IRS form number SS-4.

Aside from paying estimated federal income taxes quarterly, employers are required by the IRS to withhold federal income taxes, social security taxes, and Medicare taxes from their employees' pay. The withholdings must be forwarded to the IRS by the 15th day of the following month, by either making an electronic deposit directly to the IRS, or by making a deposit at your commercial bank, using Federal Tax Deposit Form 8109. To calculate payroll withholdings, an employer should refer to IRS Circular E, Employer's Tax Guide.

State and Local Requirements and Controls

Although the requirements for opening a bar vary from state to state, all states require a liquor license to sell alcoholic beverages at the retail level. A bar or tavern owner is a retailer. In addition, all states have regulations that govern what you can sell, where you can sell it, when and to whom you may sell it, and how you may advertise and promote it.

The type and number of licenses available also vary from state to state. The license for a bar that sells alcoholic beverages for consumption only on the licensed premises is called an *on-premise* license. There is a variety of on-premise licenses, such as restaurant, tavern, ballroom, golf course, bowling alley, and club licenses. Each type of license has special criteria that must be met. The effective term of a license is one year, and it applies to only one specific location.

All states have an Alcoholic Beverage Control (ABC) agency. In some states, only the state ABC agency issues liquor licenses. In other states, cities are allowed to issue liquor licenses, provided the state ABC agency approves the issuance of the licenses.

License States vs. Control States

There are two categories of states as regards governmental involvement in the liquor business. They are *license states* and *control states*. In a license state the sale of alcoholic beverages is conducted by private businesses. In those states, liquor, beer, and wine products are distributed by private wholesalers, which have salespeople who call on bars.

In a control state the state is in the liquor business. In those states, bars must buy their stock from state liquor stores or warehouses. There are 18 control states and each has its own regulations and ways of doing business.

Every state publishes a book, free or at normal cost, describing its liquor laws and regulations. Prospective bar owners should obtain a copy from their state ABC agency.

Liquor Licenses

In some states, new liquor licenses are difficult to obtain because they are issued on the basis of population. In other states, new licenses are readily issued as long as the applicant and the premises meet the requirements for a license. Each state has its own requirements. Applicants for liquor licenses are checked thoroughly. Of greatest concern to state liquor control boards is an applicant's ability to obey laws and be financially responsible.

Although liquor laws vary from one jurisdiction to another, they typically cover the following items:

- Types of licenses available, fees, and the application process
- Requirements for acquiring a license

- Hours and days of operation
- Proximity to churches, schools, and hospitals
- Who may be employed
- Who may not be served alcoholic beverages
- Change of ownership or managers
- Changes or alterations to the licensed premises
- Entertainment
- Adulteration of alcoholic beverages
- Advertising restrictions

The general requirements for a liquor license are:

The applicant must
- be 21 years of age or older;
- be financially responsible;
- have good moral character; and
- be an American citizen.

Before a liquor license will be issued, a bar must have a food service license, a fire permit and, if construction or renovations are necessary, a building permit.

As with all businesses, a bar must register its name with the secretary of state and comply with the state's labor laws, handicap access regulations, and tax collection regulations. For specific details as to the requirements, you should check with the appropriate agencies in your particular state.

Food Service Licenses

The name of this license may vary from state to state (Massachusetts calls it an Innholder/Common Victualler license), but the intent is the same—to ensure that you operate in a sanitary and safe manner, meeting all the provisions of the food sanitation codes. Licenses are issued for one year at a time, and you must have one in order to operate.

State and local public health authorities cooperate closely. In some locales, local health departments administer inspections and issue food service licenses subject to approval by the state public health department. In others, state public health officials administer all aspects of the sanitation code.

The typical process for obtaining a food service license is as follows:

1. Advise local officials of your proposed bar or restaurant, including

   • Building inspector

   • Planning board

   • Zoning board

2. Submit floor plans of your establishment to the local health department, which will advise you if it is necessary to submit them to the state health department. Call to make an appointment to bring in the plans for review.

   • Show the placement of all major equipment and location of sinks and restrooms, and include a list of materials to be used for floors, walls, ceilings, and work surfaces.

   • Include a copy of your proposed food and beverage menus.

3. Complete and submit a license application with the appropriate fee to the local or state health department, as directed.

4. Call the health department for a pre-opening inspection at least seven days prior to planned opening date.

5. If all goes well with the pre-opening inspection a food service license or health permit will be issued, and periodic inspections will follow.

When planning a bar or food service facility, particular attention should be paid to toilets and hand washing facilities, sewage disposal, plumbing, lighting, ventilation, dishwashing and glasswashing facilities, and all food contact surfaces. These are areas of vital concern to public health authorities.

Fire Permits

A bar or restaurant cannot open for business until it has been issued a fire permit. The state fire marshal's office and local fire departments work hand in hand, but as a rule, it is the local fire departments that do the on-site inspections.

The local fire department places a limit on the number of patrons allowed into an establishment. That capacity is determined by square footage and other factors contained in the state and local fire codes, which are modeled after the National Fire Protection Code.

Local fire departments issue permits upon passage of an inspection that includes, but is not limited to, the following items of concern:

- *Fire Extinguishers:* an adequate quantity and type with proper placement throughout the premises. They must usually be located within 75 feet from any point, have a particular rating, and be visible.

- *Exits:* There must be the proper number of exits, in the right locations, with no obstructions in the pathway, and with illuminated exit signs above them. External exit doors must swing outward and be mounted with crash bars.

- *Electrical:* All electrical work must conform to applicable building codes and be done by licensed electricians, using approved materials. There must be an adequate electrical supply to safely meet the load required by the equipment and other electrically powered systems.

- *Fire Detection:* Smoke detectors and appropriate fire suppression systems (such as sprinklers, CO_2, and dry chemical dispensers) must be in place, as well as an emergency lighting system.

- *Flammable Liquids:* The storage, use and disposal of any flammable liquids (such as cooking oils) must be by approved means. Cooking equipment that utilizes combustible liquids must be protected by fire hoods with built-in suppression systems.

- *Sprinklers:* Must not be covered, blocked, or otherwise impaired from performing as intended.

- *Storage:* Aisles of at least 36" should be provided between shelves. Approved metal containers must be provided for debris or other combustible materials.

- *Clearances:* Gas fired, and other fuel-burning equipment, must be installed with specified clearances from walls, ceilings, and floors.

- *Miscellaneous:* Chimneys, heating equipment, and vent systems must meet code requirements.

Building Permits

In most communities, it is necessary to check with several other agencies before scheduling the building inspection. Following is the usual sequence of events for obtaining a building permit and a certificate of occupancy:

- Check with the zoning board to determine whether the zoning at your proposed location will allow your type of business.

- Obtain a site approval from the planning board. This is an important step in the case of a bar, because this is when public hearings will be held and abutters may voice objection to your business. It is best to know of any objections early on.

- Next, a plan review meeting is held with both a building and fire department official present. They will review the plans in detail, paying particular attention to the structural integrity of the building, the occupancy capacity for which it is rated, fire detection systems, and conformance with all applicable building codes.

- Finally, formal application is made for a building permit.

If everything checks out well in the above stages, a building permit is issued and construction may be started. From this point on, the building inspector will make periodic inspections of the construction, to determine compliance with codes. You must use licensed electricians and plumbers.

When the construction is completed, the building inspector and the health inspector will make a final inspection. Upon passage of that inspection, a certificate of occupancy is issued to the owner of the business.

Other State or Local Departments

You may also need to contact the following state and local departments:

- *Secretary of State:* To register the name of the business, and to incorporate, if that is the legal form of business chosen.

- *Commission on the Handicapped:* To inquire about accessibility requirements for new construction and renovations.

- *Bureau of Weights and Measures:* For inspection of any scales to be used for commercial trade.

- *Department of Revenue:* For information on sales taxes or meals taxes that may have to be collected.

- *Signage Commission:* Many communities now have an agency that controls signage and requires that a permit be obtained before a sign may be installed. They are primarily concerned with the size (square footage) of the sign, its height from ground level, and the type of illumination planned for it.

- *Historical Commission:* If you plan to utilize a designated historical building for your business, you may not be able to do the things you want with it. Similarly, if you wish to establish a business within a historical district, you will have strict restrictions on what you may or may not do to the property.

- *Wetlands Commission:* If you are looking at a property for your business that contains wetlands, you may not be able to fill it in for your parking lot. Inquire first.

In recent years, water supply and septic systems have come under much tighter control, as has the disposal of hazardous materials. These are important matters to investigate when buying a property, particularly in suburban areas where wells and septic systems are common. Beware, as well, of underground fuel tanks that may have to be removed at considerable cost.

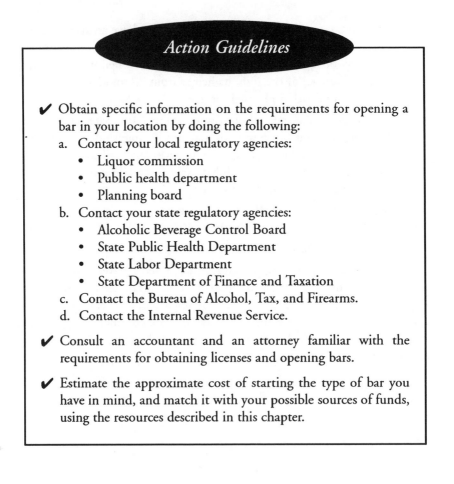

Action Guidelines

✔ Obtain specific information on the requirements for opening a bar in your location by doing the following:

   a. Contact your local regulatory agencies:
- Liquor commission
- Public health department
- Planning board

   b. Contact your state regulatory agencies:
- Alcoholic Beverage Control Board
- State Public Health Department
- State Labor Department
- State Department of Finance and Taxation

   c. Contact the Bureau of Alcohol, Tax, and Firearms.

   d. Contact the Internal Revenue Service.

✔ Consult an accountant and an attorney familiar with the requirements for obtaining licenses and opening bars.

✔ Estimate the approximate cost of starting the type of bar you have in mind, and match it with your possible sources of funds, using the resources described in this chapter.

PREPARING FOR SUCCESS

The ingredients for entrepreneurial success have been studied for a long time, but to date no one has come up with a formula that works in every case. The best you can hope for is that with diligence, training, experience, good planning, and responsible execution of your plans, you stand a chance of succeeding. And you can increase your chances by learning from the experience of others.

Why Do Some Establishments Fail?

Some people think owning a bar is a sure way to riches. Others believe bars can endure the worst of economic times and even survive poor management, because alcoholic beverages have such a high mark-up. The facts show, however, that many bars fail each year.

Eighty percent of all new businesses fail within the first five years of their existence. Hospitality businesses are no exception. As with most unsuccessful businesses, two main causes of failure stand out. One is undercapitalization and the other is lack of knowledge about the business.

Undercapitalization, which simply put means "not having enough money to do the job," usually results from not having a financial plan when entering business. Some entrepreneurs use all of their funds to buy a business and do not have enough money left to meet the first month's bills. Some overspend on new equipment or renovations rather than phase in changes on a schedule that would match their cash flow. In the event a prospective buyer or builder does not have enough capital to enter the business safely, it is best to hold off until the capital position is improved.

Lack of knowledge of the business covers a broad spectrum from not knowing one's customers to not having any training or experience in the field.

Money alone cannot buy profitability. Some investors who have adequate funds to enter a business but lack the interest or ability to manage it properly, unfortunately wind up with losses instead of profits.

Close supervision and sound policies and procedures are required. Proprietors must constantly monitor their business and look for weak spots that need improvement.

The following recommendations will help you stay in business:

- Conduct a feasibility study before buying or starting a business.
- Seek guidance from a reputable accountant and lawyer, preferably acquainted with the hospitality field.
- Broaden your knowledge of the business as much as possible through: personal research, reading trade journals and books, talking with salespeople, attending professional seminars, and taking useful courses.
- Join your local professional associations and network with other restaurants and bar owners.
- Utilize your suppliers as educational resources on new products, trends, and promotional ideas.
- Develop a financial plan (cash flow, budget) for your first year in business.
- Compare your actual performance against your plan at frequent intervals during the year.
- Control the following profit centers carefully from the outset of your business:
  - *Purchasing.* Establish specifications for each product (purveyor, brand, bottle size, maximum and minimum stock levels).
  - *Receiving.* Count and inspect all incoming shipments for proper quantity and breakage before signing invoices.
  - *Storing.* Put away all incoming shipments of liquor, beer, and wine immediately and keep it in locked storage. Issue a mini-

mum of keys to the liquor storeroom and only to supervisory or management personnel.

- *Issuing.* Record all additions to issues from inventory in an inventory book.

- *Inventory.* Take a physical inventory (actually counted) at least once a month to verify the accuracy of the balances on hand shown in the inventory book.

- *Drink mixing and serving:* Use standard recipes and standard glass sizes for all drinks.

- *Cashiering.* Make sure every drink is accounted for, according to your policies. If you want to give away a drink, fine, it is your business. But no one else should have the right to give away your profits.

• Know your customers. The better you know them individually and as a class the better you will be able to serve them. Some ways of categorizing your customers are age, sex, income, interests, type of jobs, education levels, type of transportation, and brand preferences.

• Observe your customers' spending habits. Where are they spending their money? What are they buying? How much do they tend to spend? What time do they arrive? How long do they stay? Do they come alone or with friends?

• Establish and adhere to responsible business practices. This will affect your relations with your liquor control board and your acceptance by the community.

• Keep up-to-date on liquor laws and regulations.

• Advertise effectively to attract the type of clientele you desire.

• Make your customers feel welcome. Talk to them and get feedback.

• Give your customers reasons to come back again soon. Develop a steady flow of promotional events and announce them on table tents and wall posters.

• Price your drinks competitively, according to your particular style of service. Serve high-quality drinks.

• Keep your premises clean and up-to-date.

Finally, management should conduct periodic surveys of the business to identify problems and anticipate possible causes of failure. Corrective action should be taken as soon as possible. Assess corrective actions soon after implementation to determine effectiveness and to detect any unforeseen adverse consequences of an action.

For example, suppose the ABC Lounge is losing customers to the XYZ Lounge, a new competitor that has entertainment. So, in response ABC begins to offer entertainment. After two weeks, ABC reviews the situation and finds sales are still declining, and on top of that, profits have shrunk because of the cost of the entertainment. The corrective action must be assessed. Possibly, they have engaged the wrong type of entertainment for their clientele. Or, it may be that the competitor's entertainment is not what is drawing the customers away. It might be that the quality of food or drinks at the ABC Lounge has slipped or any number of other reasons. The point is ABC must recognize that the corrective action has not achieved the desired result and modify it.

Management must be honest and objective in its appraisal of how good the business is performing. Be your severest critic, because no one else cares as much as you do about the success of your business.

Two Approaches to Entering the Business

As with most other small businesses, there are two approaches to entry: One, is to start a new bar or tavern, the other to buy an existing one. Neither approach is a sure-fire guarantee of success. However, having a knowledge of the factors involved in each can significantly improve your chances of succeeding.

Should You Start a New Business?

If you have a truly unique concept, and have (or can raise) the necessary funding, you will probably want to launch your bar as a new business. If extensive renovations are required, they can eradicate most of the savings associated with buying an existing business and oftentimes do not render the desired result.

In starting a new business, you are pioneering your concept. Everything you do will have already been done in an established business. The difference is you will be able to do it your way. However, you will have to address all of the responsibilities of a business start-up. For example, you will have to establish an organization, find a suitable location,

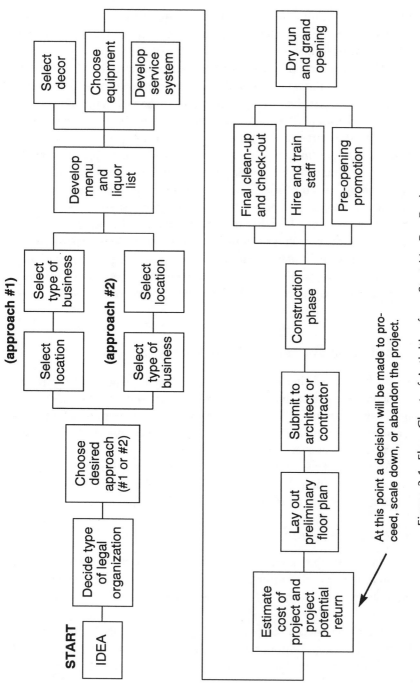

Figure 3.1: Flow Chart of Activities for a Start-Up Bar Business.

develop your menu and liquor list, determine prices, project sales, purchase equipment, select your decor, develop a service system, plan your entertainment format, and hire and train a new staff.

When all of these things are done, you will open your doors to the public and hope your new business will be a success. You can never be sure until the operation is tested in the marketplace, toe to toe against the competition.

Figure 3.1 on p. 25 depicts the typical progression of activities associated with the start-up of a bar business when adequate financing is in place. If external financing is required, you will have to plan the project up to the point of estimating its cost and potential return before approaching investors or lenders. The cost of the project must be reasonable in terms of its potential return. If the estimated costs are excessive, you will have to loop back in the process and make the changes necessary to complete the project with available funds. Consultants, experienced in the hospitality field may be engaged to assist with equipment selection and costing. The talents, financial resources, and experience of the principals make every start-up situation unique, however, the basic process tends to be the same.

Should You Buy an Existing Business?

If you buy an existing business you will have a going concern with an immediate cash flow, and you will save the start-up costs of a new business. But care must be taken to assure you do not inherit unwanted problems, such as an irreparable bad reputation, an incompetent staff, outdated equipment, or a short lease.

Arrange to have an equipment specialist accompany you when you inspect the business. Look at the age and condition of the equipment. Determine if it was cleaned well and cared for properly.

How Much Should You Pay?

The answer to this question will vary with the facts of each situation. There is no one rule of thumb. For instance, if you were considering buying a business in its entirety—a going operation with a successful track record and cash flow—it would be valued one way; whereas, if you intend to buy just the assets of a business, they would be valued quite differently. In the first case, the price would be based on the value of the assets plus the value of a proven income stream. In the second case, the price would be based solely on the value of the assets, which unless utilized properly, may or may not produce profits.

Similarly, if a business were located in an extraordinarily good location, it would command a substantial premium over the price of one in a mediocre location.

Potential buyers may use several techniques to assess an existing business and use the results to determine a high and low end of an acceptable price range. This is an area where you should work closely with your accountant. Four of the more common methods are listed below:

1. *Comparable Values of Similar Going Concerns:* This method arrives at a value based on what similar businesses have sold for.

2. *Reproduction or Replacement Value:* This method is based on the open-market cost of reproducing the assets of the business. It is most useful when only the assets of a business are being purchased.

3. *Earnings Approach:* This method focuses on the annual earnings of the business. Earnings can be used to calculate your potential return-on-investment, however, some cautions are important.

   Earnings can vary with methods of accounting. For example, in the case of sole proprietorship, if the owner did not take a salary, the business's earnings would appear much higher than they otherwise would be. Also, if economic conditions have shifted and are now declining, past performance may not be a good indicator of what can be expected in the future.

   Some people will use a multiple of annual earnings to establish a theoretical value that fits their amortization timetable. However, in the end you must regard earnings as only one measure that must be looked at alongside the others.

4. *Book Value:* Essentially this is the adjusted book value of a business, arrived at by subtracting total liabilities from total assets and adjusting for any intangibles such as goodwill. Although the data is based on a firm's most recent balance sheet, the value of the assets should be tested for fair market value, and if necessary, so restated.

What Should You Pay for Rent?

The words location, location, location dictate the value of rents. Time and place are all important. Time refers to what is happening at a location within a given period. For instance, a storefront one block away from an Olympic Village during an Olympic year will fetch a far greater rent than it would at another time. Similarly, a storefront located between two popular anchor stores in a high volume mall would garner a higher rent than a store in a less desirable location.

Rent is also influenced by factors other than the traffic count. The age of a building and the prestige value of its address, as well as the provision of amenities, such as heat, light, water, parking, and snow removal, will affect rents. When expenses such as property taxes, insurance and maintenance are paid by the lessee, the lease is referred to as a triple net lease. A National Restaurant Association publication, *Restaurant Industry Operations Report, 1993*, shows occupancy costs (which include rent, property taxes, and insurance) for full-menu, table service restaurants that sell both food and beverages averaged 4.5% to 9.5% of total sales.

It is important when planning, to be conservative in estimating total sales so as to not elevate expenses that are forecast as a percentage of sales.

Evaluating an Opportunity

It is vital that you research a business carefully before buying it. Figure 3.2 is a checklist for surveying an existing beverage establishment. It can also be used as a guide or reference list at many stages of the planning process. It will remind you of things that might easily be overlooked.

Professional Assistance

In addition to a checklist, use experts to help you evaluate the business. Talk to bankers, suppliers, and repairmen. They can give you information about many aspects of the business. Also talk to patrons, neighbors, and anyone else who may have information about the business. Try to find out how the business has been doing in regard to sales, public image, and customer satisfaction. But most of all, be sure to get your accountant and lawyer involved at this stage of your evaluation.

Insist that your accountant be permitted to examine the official books of the business. Check on outstanding bills and tax obligations if you buy the business in its entirety. If deposits for future business (functions booked in advance) have been accepted by the current owner, adjustments should be made during the closing process. The tax status of the business should be examined carefully. Have all taxes been paid or are their tax issues to be resolved with the IRS?

Closing the Deal

Engage a lawyer who is familiar with the hospitality industry. If you need a referral, contact your local bar association, which can give you several names. Your lawyer should be present at all signings and should review all documents before you sign them. You will be encountering contractual matters that are beyond the ability of the average layperson to cope with. Make any agreements contingent upon your acquiring the necessary licenses and permits, because without your licenses and permits you will not be able to open for business.

Selecting Your Legal Form of Business

There are basically three legal forms of business from which you may choose: the sole proprietorship, the partnership, and the corporation. Each has its advantages and disadvantages. At issue will be, how much money you have to invest, how much personal involvement in the business you wish to undertake, tax implications, liability and disclosure requirements. Which legal form of business is best for you is a matter that should be worked out with your lawyer and accountant.

Sole Proprietorship

The sole proprietorship is popular because it gives the owner complete domination over a business. The owner can make the rules and set the policies, take time off at will or work long hours. Best of all, the owner gets to keep all of the after-tax profits, and the profits are taxed as if they were personal income. The idea of no boss or committee meetings is very appealing. In addition, the owner enjoys prestige, hires and fires people, and has final authority for everything.

The other side of the sole proprietorship picture is that the owner must carry the entire financial burden of the business and be competent at all of the roles he or she assumes. The greatest disadvantage of a sole proprietorship is its unlimited liability. Everything of value that the proprietor owns is at risk if the business fails or is sued.

Partnership

Small partnerships enjoy some of the advantages of a sole proprietorship except that everything you own, do, or earn is shared with one or more partners. There are two basic types of partnerships, *general* and *limited.*

Areas to Evaluate	Comments
1. Beverage purchasing and receiving procedures	
2. Beverage storing and issuing methods	
3. Bar equipment and layout a. Location of equipment b. Maintenance of equipment c. Efficient placement	
4. Functional aspects of beverage dispensing equipment a. Cleanability b. Attractive design c. Ease of operation	
5. Drink preparation methods a. Quality control—recipes b. Use of premixes c. Portion control d. Showmanship	
6. Inventory selections a. Item popularity b. Product availability c. Price range	
7. Personnel a. Staffing b. Duties and responsibilities c. Grooming d. Uniforms e. Productivity f. Morale	
8. Labor a. Turnover of employees b. Training on the job c. Overtime policies	
9. Bar costs a. Standard drink recipes b. Inventory control records c. Pilferage control d. Calculation of bar cost percentages	
10. Drink presentation methods a. Size of drinks b. Garnishing the drinks c. Cashiering the system	

Figure 3.2: Checklist for Surveying an Existing Beverage Establishment.

11. Service system
    a. Drink ordering
    b. Pick up system
    c. Guest check controls
    d. Drink delivery system

12. Lounge
    a. Number of cocktail servers
    b. Tables per station
    c. Style of service
    d. Decor
    e. Type of clientele
    f. Average guest check size

13. China, glassware, utensils, paper supplies
    a. Back-up inventory supply
    b. Inventory-taking procedures
    c. Reorder policies

14. Advertising, sales, promotion
    a. Types of ads, frequency
    b. Media used
    c. Method for developing ads

15. Sanitation
    a. Policies
    b. Training
    c. Equipment
    d. Method of supervision

16. Safety
    a. Fire extinguishing equipment
    b. Fire exits
    c. Fire retardant materials
    d. Emergency lighting

17. Communications
    a. Lines of authority
    b. Supervision
    c. Policy manual

18. Accounting Controls
    a. Food cost controls
    b. Beverage cost controls
    c. Labor cost controls

19. Physical appearance of property
    a. Building
    b. Furniture, fixtures and equipment
    c. Obsolescence factor

In a *general partnership*, all partners have unlimited liability. In a *limited partnership* there must be at least one general partner who runs the business and has unlimited liability, and an unrestricted number of limited partners who have limited liability and are not required to take an active role in the operations of the business.

Partnerships function best when the partners have complimentary talents and each brings financial resources to the business. A partnership agreement should be drawn up by an attorney and signed by all partners. At the very least, it should include the names of all partners, the amount of each partner's investment, the share of the firm's profits to which each partner will be entitled, the role and responsibilities of each partner in the operations of the business, and what will happen in the event a partner dies or wants to sell his or her ownership share.

Be very careful about the individuals with whom you become a partner. One partner's actions may jeopardize a business and create a liability that must be shared by all partners. Unless you need the skills or the funds of others to launch your business, you have no reason to consider the partnership form of business.

Corporation

The Supreme Court defines a corporation as "a fictitious person." Consequently, because you are a real person, you cannot be a corporation. A corporation is a separate entity from yourself. You can, however, be a stockholder, a director, an officer, or an employee of a corporation. Three or more persons can obtain a corporate charter, elect a board of directors, which directs the corporation, and appoint officers to run it. Following is a list of advantages of incorporating:

- Your liability is limited to your investment in the corporation (unless you misuse corporate funds or facilities).

- Your personal assets are protected from seizure or attachment by corporate creditors or lawsuits.

- Filing a Sub-Chapter S election allows gains and losses to flow directly through to stockholders, so that they can be treated as personal income. (In this respect the Sub-Chapter S corporation is like a partnership.)

- Raising additional capital for growth or expansion is easier than with a proprietorship or partnership.

- Stock can be used as collateral for loans, whereas proprietorships and partnerships may have to use their personal assets.

Raising Additional Capital

This is where the corporate form of business has a distinct advantage over other forms. A corporation may sell additional shares of stock without affecting the workings of the company because its owners are legally separated from the operations of the company. A corporation can also obtain debt capital from professional lending institutions.

A sole proprietor cannot sell stock and must borrow additional capital on the strength of his or her personal and business reputation. If you are an established member of your business community with an upstanding reputation and are well-networked in local financial circles, borrowing as a private individual should not present a problem. However, if you are new to a community, you will find it more difficult.

Partnerships have the ability to bring new partners with investment capital into the firm. However, finding the right persons with whom to associate is not always an easy matter. Extreme caution must be exercised because of the unlimited liability feature of a general partnership.

Selecting a Location and Property

The checklist in Figure 3.3 (pp. 34-35) can be useful when examining sites. Using a tape recorder to store information as you evaluate potential sites is a good idea. Not all items are applicable in every situation.

Selecting a Name

The actual process of registering a business name is an easy matter. Simply obtain the appropriate forms from the secretary of state's office (in your state capital), fill them out specifying your desired names, and return them to the secretary of state with a check for the stipulated fee. It is wise to submit three desired names in their order of preference. The names will be screened through a computer, and if no one else has already registered the name you want, you will get it. That is the legal side of selecting a name.

The public relations side is equally important. Thoughtful consideration should be given to your name because it can serve many purposes.

Address of Site _____ Present Owner or Agent _____

City/State/Zip _____ Address_____

Lot No._____ City/State/Zip_____

Map Ref._____ Tel. _____

Date of Inspection _____ Asking Price _____

Physical Features of the Land

Size:	Approach/visibility:
Shape:	Accessibility to target:
Slope:	Clearance:
Expansion possibilities:	Zoning:
Utilities :	Nearby hazard or blights:
Water, gas, electricity, sewers	Parking possibilities
Soil conditions: perc tests, drainage	Snow removal or storage space

Economic and Community Features

Economic trend:	Wage trends:
Public transportation:	Competition:
Local attractions:	Income levels:
Civic promotional/agencies:	Seasonal features:
Labor supply:	Major highways nearby:
Population (number and make-up):	Fire and police protection:
Daily traffic:	Food and beverage suppliers:
Auto count:	
Pedestrian count:	

Figure 3.3: Site Analysis Checklist

Physical Features of the Structure

This is a partial list. Your real estate agent can supply you with additional information.

Perimeter dimensions: Type of siding and roofing:

No. of rooms and sizes   Electrical service (amps, phase):

Traffic flow lines: Gas service (LP or natural, size):

No. of restrooms: Sewer (municipal or septic tank):

Flooring materials: Water (munic. or well, volume):

Storage possibilities: Handicap accessibility:

Insulation: Heating/ventilation/AC:

Laws and Restrictions

Zoning of property: Building height and set-back:

Land-use and environmental laws: Requirement:

Permits and licenses needed: Lighting and signage:

Building restrictions: Other requirement:

Wetland restrictions:

Taxes

Property tax: Meals and lodging tax:

Income or business tax: State sales tax:

Assessment percentage: Water and sewer tax:

City sales tax:

Cost of Property

Land: Necessary improvements:

Building: Total investment:

Data may be obtained from tax offices, registry of deeds books, town or city clerks, real estate agents and brokers, highway departments, chambers of commerce, as well as on-site inspections.

Some examples of the functions of names are:

- Cap'n Jacks—suggests a nautical atmosphere
- The Bridge Street Cafe—tells you where it is
- The Music Box Lounge—tells you they feature music
- Rock & Bock Pub—indicates a pub with loud music for young people.

Think about the message you want your name to convey in terms of your target market, its wants, and expectations.

Managing Risk

Acquiring adequate insurance, training your staff, and setting sound company policies are the three main ways to manage risk. A successful risk management program must incorporate all three. It is advisable to have an insurance agent or broker design a complete insurance program for your business. Types of insurance available include:

- *Liquor Liability.* Protects against suits resulting from damages or injuries to others by a person who became intoxicated in your establishment.
- *Property Damage.* Covers buildings, inventory, equipment, and fixtures against loss due to fire, smoke, explosion, or vandalism.
- *General Comprehensive Liability.* Covers claims for bodily injury and property damage due to an accident.
- *Personal Injury Liability.* Covers lawsuits due to false arrest, libel, slander, defamation of character, and personal injuries.
- *Automobile Liability.* Covers damages or injuries that employees incur while driving their car or a company car in the performance of company business.
- *Product Liability.* Covers against lawsuits based on damages or injuries resulting from a product that you served.
- *Fire.* Covers damages to other buildings from a fire that originated on your property.
- *Workers' Compensation.* Covers employees' medical and rehabilitation costs for work-related injuries.

- *Business Interruption.* Reimburses you for expenses incurred and for revenues and profits lost as a result of unintended interruption of your business due to fire, major theft, or illness of a key employee.
- *Bonds.* Covers against lawsuits for financial loss incurred by others due to an act or default of an employee or to some contingency over which the principal may have no control.

Some carriers specialize in insuring beverage establishments. Their rates will vary according to the type of business, condition of the premises, degree of exposure to risks, and your risk management program.

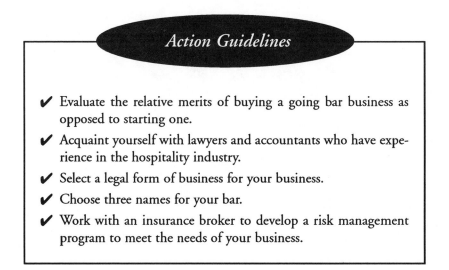

Action Guidelines

✔ Evaluate the relative merits of buying a going bar business as opposed to starting one.

✔ Acquaint yourself with lawyers and accountants who have experience in the hospitality industry.

✔ Select a legal form of business for your business.

✔ Choose three names for your bar.

✔ Work with an insurance broker to develop a risk management program to meet the needs of your business.

Chapter
4

PLANNING FOR PROFITS

The Cornerstone of Planning is the Business Plan

A business plan can serve a number of purposes, including persuading someone to support your project financially. However, its first and foremost value is to focus your thinking on what you wish to achieve and how you intend to do it. Preparing a business plan forces you to think through every aspect of your prospective business. If there are weaknesses, they will become evident as you work through the plan. Beyond that, your business plan can serve as a road map through your start-up period and be a reference point against which you can compare your actual results.

When preparing your business plan, it is essential that you be sure of your facts and be prepared to defend their validity. Investors and lenders will consider false or incomplete information as unreliable or deceptive. Apart from that, inaccurate information will mislead you in evaluating your project's chances for success.

A well-written business plan will convey to its readers the impression that you can think clearly and have the ability to successfully run a business.

Estimating Your Start-Up Costs

There are numerous sources for information on costs. Equipment suppliers will provide you with working figures on bar and food service equipment. Commercial real estate agents can supply cost data and advice on suitable properties. Architects and contractors, interested in your business, will give you ballpark figures as you consider the feasibility of your project. Distributors of food, liquor, beer and wine can assist you in estimating inventory costs. Since you are a potential customer, it is in their best interest to help you with your early planning. Wherever possible, cross check information with more than one source.

If your business is a sole proprietorship or partnership you will have limited capital. Consequently, the matter of estimating start-up costs will happen in stages, starting with ballpark figures. As your ideas become better defined, your estimates will become more realistic. At each stage of the process, you must answer the question, "Can I afford it?" If you believe you can, then you will proceed to obtain final figures and that might entail hiring a consultant to develop a reliable estimate for you.

If you do not feel you can afford the project, according to the ballpark figures, you must go back to square one and scale down your ideas or abandon the project.

Should your business be a corporation, you will have the opportunity to raise unlimited funds through the sale of stock. However, your potential investors will scrutinize your business plan carefully and will want to be convinced of the business's chances of success and the anticipated rate of return on investment.

The format for business plans can vary. But, certain sections of information commonly appear in all business plans. An outline of a typical business plan is shown in Figure 4.1, and is followed by detailed explanations of the type of information that might appear in each section. A sample business plan for a bar and grill appears in Appendix A.

Description of a Business Plan

The Cover Page

The Cover Page tells the reader who you are. It should include

- the name of your company
- the date the business plan is issued
- the name and title of the principal person submitting the plan
- the address and telephone number of the business.

Cover Page
Table of Contents
Statement of Purpose

Part One: The Business
- Description of the Business
- Background of the Business
- The Company's Mission Statement
- The Concept
- Location
- Industry Trends
- Other Resources
- The Management
- Objectives and Financial Expectations
- Product and Service
- Pricing and Profitability
- Product Life Cycle
- Market Analysis
- Competition
- Customers
- Marketing Strategy
- Personnel
- Risk
- Loan Request and Anticipated Benefits
- Summary of Part One

Part Two: Financial Projections
- Start-Up Requirements
- Estimated Annual Sales
- List of Furniture, Fixtures, and Equipment
- Leasehold Improvements
- Sources and Uses of Funds
- Income Statement for First Year
- Projected Income Statement—Month by Month
- Cash Flow Statement by Month
- Daily Break-Even Analysis
- Conclusion and Summary of Part Two

Part Three: Supporting Documents
(All legal and professional documents that support the information contained in Parts One and Two. In addition, the following should be included: personal résumés of all principals, the personal balance sheets, credit reports, letters of recommendation, letters of intent, copies of leases and contracts, and any other applicable documents that will strengthen the plan.)

Figure 4.1: Outline of a Business Plan

- The number of the plan (if you are submitting multiple copies of the plan).

The Table of Contents

The Table of Contents lists what is contained and where it appears in your business plan. The page numbers should not be inserted until after the plan is completed in every other respect.

You should number the pages using chapter and page numbers, such as 1.1, 1.2, 1.3. for chapter one; and 2.1, 2.2, 2.3 for chapter two; and so on. This allows you to add pages at the end of each chapter at the last minute without having to renumber the entire document. For clarity, always start new sections on a new page. Business plans will typically run 20 or more pages.

Statement of Purpose

Explain, in a summarized way, what the rest of the report will cover in detail. Answer the Who, What, When, Where, and How questions.

- Who is the report about? Who is asking for the loan?
- What is the business? What is your legal form of ownership (sole proprietorship, partnership, corporation, Sub-Chapter S corporation)?
- How much funding is sought?
- What will the funds be used for?
- What benefits will result to the business from the use of the funds?
- How will the borrowed funds be repaid? If you are seeking outside funding, this information will be of great interest to the lender. If you are preparing the business plan for your own use, it should be of equal interest for you to know the business's prospects for achieving your desired profit objective.

Part One: The Business

In this section, you will describe the business and tell what it will do, and how it will do it.

Description of the Company. Provide your business's name and intended starting date. State the products and services, days and hours of business, the names of the investors, and their roles in the business.

Background of the Business. Describe the idea and your research findings from surveys and interviews. Indicate why the findings support your proposed business.

The Company's Mission Statement. This is a statement of your overall goal for the company, throughout its lifetime, as you now see it.

The Concept. Describe the concept in detail and explain its uniqueness. Tell how your business will fit into the marketplace and focus on the desirability of your concept. Photographs and illustrations are useful in highlighting key items of interest. Lengthy exhibits should be placed in the appendix at the back of the business plan and referenced in the body of the text.

Location. Indicate why you have chosen the proposed site and describe its features. Use your Property Analysis Checklist to obtain this information.

Industry Trends. Describe what industry analysts predict for the next year or two. Reference the sources from which the information was obtained, such as the National Restaurant Association, your state hospitality association, the Licensed Beverage Industry Association, the Bureau of Alcohol, Tax & Firearms, trade journals, census data, etc.

Other Resources. For financial resources list your food and equipment suppliers and state their credit terms. Also list professional resources— lawyer, accountant, banker, insurance agent, consultant.

The Management. Describe your management team. Cover the personal histories of the owners and top employees. State their training and experience and point out how they are suited to the duties and responsibilities they will be assuming. Their proposed salaries should be stipulated as well as anything about them that will enhance the business's chances for success.

Objectives and Financial Expectations. Enumerate your short-term and long-term goals for sales, customer acceptance, growth, and expansion. Tell where you want the business to go. Relate what you wish to achieve. Stress quality, profits, return on investment, and public service. Your objectives should be feasible, understandable, and realistic in terms of your resources.

Describe the benefits that investors and lenders may expect to realize when the business's near- and long-term objectives are met. The point here is to convince potential investors or lenders that all aspects of the project have been carefully considered and that the idea makes sense. Be accurate and thorough.

Product and Service. Differentiate your product and service from that of your competitors; describe its benefits. Here is where you inform the reader how the business will fill a market niche and meet the needs of your target market. Stress your competitive advantages. If your concept or product is based upon any proprietary secrets, such as recipes, you will want to protect them by asking investors and lenders to sign a nondisclosure agreement.

Pricing and Profitability. Explain your pricing strategy and its profit generating potential. Relate your prices to costs as well as your competitors' strategy. Use the profit potential to estimate the pay-back period for investors and lenders. Copies of price lists should be included in the Appendix.

Product Life Cycle. Describe the expected life cycle for your concept or product in the targeted marketing area. If your concept is one that has a high front end acceptance (such as trendy dance clubs), but has a limited life expectancy, point out the quick payback and high earnings potential.

Market Analysis. Define your market clearly and include charts where applicable. This section describes the market situation as it currently exists and must leave no doubt in the investors' or lenders' mind that the proposed business is appropriate for the market.

Discuss any economic conditions or market changes that may be taking place. Tell how they will benefit the business. Indicate the size of the marketing area and its potential for future growth. Detail your strengths and emphasize your marketing plans as much as your product. Point out any unexploited opportunities you recognize.

You should be realistic and identify any weaknesses you or the business may have, because the business plan is for your edification as well. Describe the ways you plan to eliminate or improve upon the weaknesses. This may be the first test of how well suited you are for the business.

Competition. Identify your five or six nearest competitors. Elucidate the process by which you obtained information about your competitors to give your findings credibility. Tell what they offer, how they advertise (frequency, type of media used, and size of advertisements). Show how that compares with your plans. Indicate the competition's strengths and weaknesses and explain how your marketing strategy addresses them.

Customers. Detail the demographics of your targeted clientele—who they are, where they live, their level of education, their income bracket, their spending habits, and their wants and needs as evidenced by research. Describe their motivation to patronize your establishment. What benefits will they receive? Why can you expect they will be attracted to your business?

Marketing Strategy. This part of your business plan will guide you as you respond to business conditions and opportunities. It can make the difference between mediocrity and the achievement of your goals. Your marketing strategy tells how you intend to position your business in the customers' mind and how, by contrast, you can reposition your competitors.

Detail the segment of the market you are targeting to reach and the market share you expect to capture. Describe the selling and advertising tactics you will use to accomplish your goals. List your outside resources—public relations agencies, ad agencies, media—and sales promotional campaigns you intend to utilize and who will be responsible for these areas.

Personnel. Describe your hours and days of business, and your style of service. These factors will reflect how many of each type of employee you will need, and the skills required. An organizational chart accompanied by a proposed personnel schedule could be included here along with estimated payroll costs.

Risk. Show that you understand the risks of the business and have plans for managing them. These might include specialized training for employees, insurance programs, and cost controls.

Loan Request and Anticipated Benefits. (This section is used when seeking external funding and should state the sum being applied for, an itemized list of the intended uses of the funds, and the benefits that will be realized from their utilization. The display of sources and uses of funds will be restated in the Financial Projections of Part Two.)

Summary of Part One

The summary consists of a few paragraphs that capsulize the contents of Part One. They should tell who you are, what you want to do, how you plan to do it, when and where, what it will cost, why it is feasible, what are the benefits, and where applicable, how much you want to borrow.

Financial Projections and Supporting Documents

The financial statements that compose Part Two of the business plan will be discussed in greater detail in Chapter 8.

The supporting documents section may include market survey data, drawings and layouts; all legal and professional documents that support the information contained in Parts One and Two; as well as credit reports, letters of recommendation, letters of intent, copies of leases, contracts, and any other documents that will strengthen the plan.

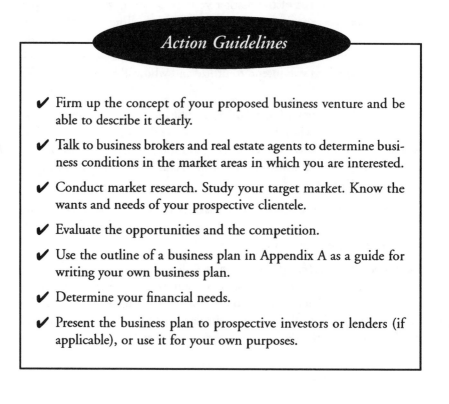

Action Guidelines

✔ Firm up the concept of your proposed business venture and be able to describe it clearly.

✔ Talk to business brokers and real estate agents to determine business conditions in the market areas in which you are interested.

✔ Conduct market research. Study your target market. Know the wants and needs of your prospective clientele.

✔ Evaluate the opportunities and the competition.

✔ Use the outline of a business plan in Appendix A as a guide for writing your own business plan.

✔ Determine your financial needs.

✔ Present the business plan to prospective investors or lenders (if applicable), or use it for your own purposes.

FACILITIES AND EQUIPMENT PLANNING

Your facilities, equipment, and layout will depend upon your product—food, drinks, entertainment, and service. All decisions you make, as you plan your facilities and equipment, should be focused on delivering the best possible product to your targeted clientele.

Consider your atmosphere, as well—do you want to be perceived as a high-energy bar with lots of activity and loud music or as a sedate lounge with comfortable seating and soft background music? Once you understand your target clientele's wants and needs and have clearly defined your product, you are ready to design your facility.

Determining Your Equipment Needs

There are several ways to determine your equipment needs. One is to hire an architect who specializes in restaurants and bars to plan and design, and build your facility. The architect will engage subcontractors to design each of the specialized areas of the project, a common practice for large jobs.

If yours is a small, uncomplicated project, such as adding a bar in an existing room in your restaurant, you can act as your own contractor. Fortunately, equipment vendors are very willing to help businesses calculate their needs and lay out a facility. They have the required expertise and are acquainted with the latest products on the market. You can benefit from the experience they bring from other projects. And if your funds are tight, they can help you work within budget by suggesting alternatives.

In order for vendors to work successfully with you, however, they must have exact data regarding the size and shape of the rooms involved, the seating capacity, and your products and services.

Should You Buy or Lease Equipment?

On occasion a business will have the opportunity to lease a particular piece of equipment. There are valid reasons for leasing and for buying equipment, but they vary from business to business and from time to time. Consequently, there is not a single answer on deciding between leasing and buying. It is important to understand the advantages and disadvantages of each course of action as shown in Figure 5.1 (p. 49).

Perhaps the most important realization when considering leasing is that "nothing is free." Everything you buy or lease has a price that includes all expenses, plus a profit for the supplier. The main reason many people lease equipment is they just don't have the money to buy it.

Another reason for at least considering leasing is as a hedge when a new business is uncertain of its future. Assuming a short-term lease, the lessee can terminate business with minimal losses as opposed to a business that buys everything and gets stuck with a lot of money tied up in used equipment. It should be noted that used food and beverage equipment is plentiful and brings very little money at auction.

Laying Out an Efficient Floor Plan

The physical layout of a beverage establishment will have a direct relationship to its profitability. Waiters and waitresses must be able to move quickly as they take orders and deliver drinks. Tight aisles and poor table arrangements can slow service and irritate guests.

Your layout should appear friendly and inviting. It should excite guests and make them want to come in and stay longer. Guests must get a pleasing view the instant they enter, for at this moment, the tone of their entire stay is very often set. A good layout will have efficient service aisles and adequate access aisles for customers to approach and leave their tables with relative ease. Restrooms should be reasonably located so as to be seen from most seating areas. Entering guests should have some free space by the entryway from which they can orient themselves and absorb the ambiance for a moment. The bar should be conveniently located so guests

BUYING

Advantages	Disadvantages
Buyer accumulates valuable assets.	Equipment will eventually wear out and need to be replaced by the buyer.
Buyer can depreciate a portion of the cost each year.	Buyer assumes the responsibility of maintaining and servicing the equipment.
Interest expense for installment payments is tax deductible.	

LEASING

Advantages	Disadvantages
Lease payments are tax deductible as business operating expenses.	Loss of depreciation.
Lessor may maintain and service the equipment for the lessee.	At end of the lease you do not own the equipment.
Lessor usually supplies brand new models and updates equipment periodically.	The built-in charge for service may be more than you would otherwise have paid for it.
Service calls on leased equipment are usually given priority over others.	

Figure 5.1: Lease or Buy.

will not have to travel a crowded or possibly embarrassing route to sit there. Figure 5.2 (p. 50) provides guidelines for a good layout.

In designing your floor plan, consider the efficiency of your bar operations. When and how often will your bar have to be stocked? From where will the supplies come? Will guest service be affected at those times? How much product will you carry at the bar? What control routines must be observed in regard to the storage and issuance of beverage supplies? The answers to these questions will determine the location of your storeroom and the size and placement of your bar.

Figure 5.2:
Guidelines For Bar and Lounge Layouts

1. Allow incoming guests to have a view of your lounge that will immediately give them the flavor of the atmosphere.

2. Avoid congestion around doorways and traffic lanes.

3. Divide large spaces into smaller, intimate areas, through the use of walls, planters, and decorator panels.

4. Use contrasting colors or materials to give smaller areas an atmosphere of their own.

5. Consider traffic paths to be used when resupplying the bar during busy periods. Avoid inconveniencing guests.

6. Provide access aisles for service personnel to deliver drinks.

7. Vary your seating clusters, so that you can handle singles, couples, and larger groups of customers.

8. Consider using folding doors to create private rooms or to close off empty areas at quiet times.

9. Plan cocktail pickup stations so that they create the least distraction or inconvenience to guests at your cash bar.

10. Lay out your bar to save steps and to be operable by a minimum staff during a slow period.

11. Install intercom systems if the bar is connected to other food or lodging facilities.

12. Fire exits and safety equipment should be easily accessible.

13. Restroom signs should be visible from most points in the lounge.

14. In colder climates, ample facilities for coat hanging should be provided.

15. Plan bar equipment so as to allow for expansion of business with a minimum of structural changes.

16. Arrange bar equipment in efficient work centers to enhance work simplification techniques and reduce stretching, reaching, turning, and other fatiguing movements.

17. Incorporate the latest equipment models available in your bar design. This gives you the most up-to-date features and puts off obsolescence.

18. Choose easily cleanable materials for equipment surfaces as well as for floors, walls, and furniture.

19. Provide sanitary and restroom facilities for employees in your plans.

20. Service bars should be located as close to the point of service as possible.

Above all, seating must be comfortable. Few people will tolerate uncomfortable seats more than once. The height of tables and chairs should be conducive to relaxing. The sizes, colors, shapes, textures, and fabrics will all send a message to your guests. Try to select a harmonious variety of seats, booths, banquettes, and tables to maximize the interest level of you decor.

Where Should the Entertainment Go?

Too often entertainers are relegated to a corner, simply because it was considered dead space. Unfortunately in those instances, the entertainment is not able to serve its full potential. Entertainment can entice customers to stay longer or come back again soon, but it can only do this if it is well placed. Consider this issue carefully and locate your entertainment where it can be enjoyed by the most customers.

Designing Your Bar

When developing a bar design, two basic questions must be answered, "What types of beverages will be served?" and "How many customers will have to be served at one time?" The answer to those two questions will form the basis of any bar layout.

The types of beverages will dictate what equipment is required, the styles of glasses needed, what is needed to prepare specialty drinks (ice cream, coffee, slush), the amount of refrigerated storage needed and whether to serve draught or bottled beer.

The number of customers will determine the quantity and size of the equipment and the necessary amount of ice, glasses, glass storage space, and serving stations required. And since every beverage begins with a clean, sterile glass, an appropriate glass washing station is always a critical design element.

After equipment sizes and quantities have been determined, the equipment has to be arranged to conform to the flow of the beverages and glasses to and from the serving stations. A serving station is defined as the area and equipment used by a bartender to mix and dispense the variety of beverages required. A small bar can use a single serving station, staffed by one server. The larger the number of customers to be served, the larger the bar and the more stations are required for efficient operation.

Oftentimes, in larger operations, a serving station is located at one or both ends of a bar with mixing and dispensing duties shared by the bartender and a server. The ideal bar design takes into account the flow of beverages from the time they are mixed and dispensed, through consumption by the customer, to the return of soiled glasses to be washed, air-dried, and stored.

Again, efficiency is always a consideration. How can a beverage order be prepared with the fewest number of steps? Where should the cocktail mixing station be in relation to the beer dispensing stations and in relation to the cash register? Will any specialty drinks have to be prepared and what is needed for them? How much floor space in relation to total space available should be dedicated to the bar operation? What is the budget? Will equipment cutbacks be necessary in order to meet budget constraints?

When a bar designer thinks about efficiency, uses common sense, and "acts out" the workings of the operation, it will become clear in the planning stage what equipment is required and where it should be placed. In essence a good bar layout is no different than an efficient kitchen or office layout.

After a bar layout has been designed, the next step is to select a vendor. That choice will be based on the brand of equipment that will best satisfy the requirements of the design. Equipment may be custom manufactured, but, custom manufacturing is often more costly and larger than modular equipment.

The modular concept, pioneered by Perlick Corporation, is based on manufacturing products whose final assembly is determined by a customer's specific requirements. With more than 275 serving station modules from which to choose Perlick can match custom specifications in less than three weeks from receipt of a customer's layout and order. Serving station modules can be mated with other free standing cabinets, such as glass frosters, bottle coolers and glass washers, to create a customized total beverage center. Figure 5.3 is a sample of a Perlick layout.

Bar equipment is available from a number of sources. However, dealing with numerous suppliers means coordinating those purchases to assure everything is going to fit and look uniform. Professional buyers prefer to buy as much equipment as meets their needs, from a single source. By doing so, they have to deal with only one purchase order and one freight shipment.

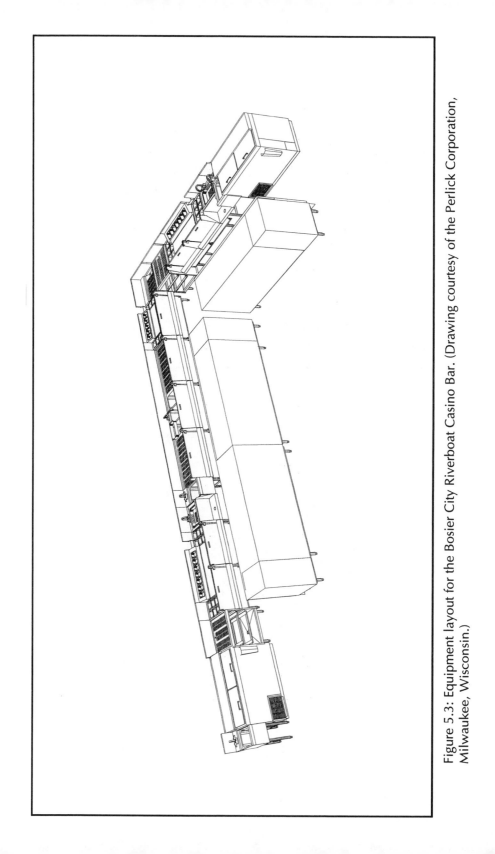

Figure 5.3: Equipment layout for the Bosier City Riverboat Casino Bar. (Drawing courtesy of the Perlick Corporation, Milwaukee, Wisconsin.)

Equipping Your Bar

All purchases of equipment should be made on the basis of 1) how well they satisfy your operational needs, and 2) how well they serve your patrons' wants and needs. Figure 5.4 illustrates an efficient beverage center.

Ask yourself the following questions before making a final purchase decision.

- Do you really need the item? Will it improve your production or service systems?
- Is it the right size? Will it do the job you expect in terms of volume, speed, and quality?
- Is it safe and sanitary?
- Will it blend in well with the rest of your equipment? Does it have a good appearance?

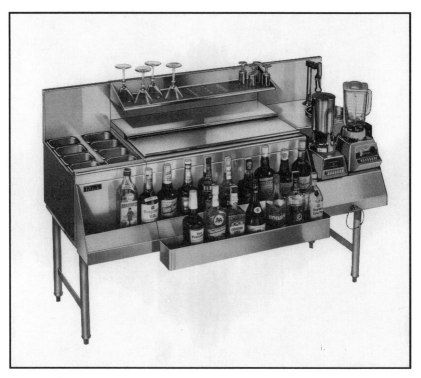

Figure 5.4: A Top Shelf beverage center with accessories. (Photo courtesy of the Perlick Corporation, Milwaukee, Wisconsin.)

- Can it be serviced easily, and what type of warranty does the seller or manufacturer offer?

- Will it fit in your available space?

- How much will the utility hook-ups and installation cost? Do you have the required electrical phase and voltage and water pressure?

- Is its cost reasonable, in relation to the answers to the above questions?

The size of your bar, its style of service and liquor list, as well as your budget will determine the type, size, and quantity of equipment you will select. See Figure 5.5 for a generic equipment list for a typical bar.

Figure 5.5:

Typical List of Under Bar and Back Bar Equipment

Sinks, 3 compartment	Ice Chest with Cold Plate
Drainboards	Bottle Wells
Speed Racks	Ice Cube Maker
Overhead Glass Rack	Ice Crusher or Flaker
Glass Chiller	Glass Washer
Beer Tap	Glass Storage Rack
Beer Mug Froster	Liquor Display Shelves
Keg Beer Cooler	Back Bar Liquor Storage Cabinets
Bottled Beer Cooler	Speed Gun Soda System
Cash Register	Cocktail Stations
Ice Cream Cabinet	Condiment Trays

How to Size Equipment

Sizing of equipment is done by calculating the volume of output during your peak periods and finding a model with the appropriate capability. You will have to refer to manufacturers' catalogs. Allow for growth of your business by reducing the manufacturers' claimed output by 30%. The following example illustrates the steps involved in selecting an ice-maker for a bar.

Selecting an Ice Maker

Step 1: Examine your liquor list to determine the various types of drinks you will be serving and the sizes of the glassware you will be using.

Step 2: Estimate the total number of drinks you will serve on a peak business day by multiplying your expected number of customers by the average number of drinks a customer consumes.

No. of Customers x Avg. No. of Drinks per Customer = Total No. of Drinks

Step 3: Multiply the total number of drinks (calculated in Step 2) by the average volume of ounces of ice your drinks will contain. Convert the total number of ounces of ice required to pounds by dividing by 16 giving you the capacity in pounds your machine will need to produce on a peak business day.

$$\frac{\text{Total No. Drinks x Avg. No. of Oz. of Ice Per Drink}}{16} = \text{Lbs. of Ice Req'd}$$

Step 4: Refer to ice-maker specifications in equipment catalog and match them up to the capacity that you need.

The Bar

A typical bar has three components: 1) the front bar, 2) the under bar, and 3) the back bar. The front bar is where the customers sit and drink. The under bar is the array of equipment installed on the rear underside of the bar, the production center. The back bar is comprised of the shelving on top, where premium liquors are displayed, and the cabinets underneath, where reserve liquor bottles are stored. Sometimes equipment, such as beer coolers, is built into the back bar.

Due to its size, the front bar is usually prefabricated in sections and stained off-premises then brought to the establishment for final assembly.

Special attention should be given to the design of the bar, because of its major contribution to the decor and ambiance of an establishment. For appearance and ease of cleaning bar equipment should be modularized as much as possible.

Lounge Evaluation and Improvement

The best of plans for a successful lounge may require fine tuning once they are in operation. Keep a constant watch for areas needing improvement. Look for overcrowding, inefficient traffic flow, poor sound control, or bored customers.

The effect of these conditions may be customers leaving earlier than planned and perhaps not returning. Problem areas cannot be ignored. Improving a lounge requires the cooperation of bar personnel. Department meetings should be held to discuss problems, objectives, and solutions. Make a practice of evaluating your lounge periodically.

Designing a Service System

The easiest way to design a service system is to put yourself in your customer's shoes and walk through the process of entering a bar or lounge, taking your seat, placing your order, and being served. Then put yourself in a bartender's or waitperson's shoes and walk through the process of greeting the customer, taking their order, turning it in or preparing it, picking it up, and delivering it to the customer.

In your mind's eye you will envision every step of the service system from order-taking to cashiering. Imagine it is opening night and a party of six people just walked through your front door. What happens next? You may have to do this several times, to make certain you haven't left out any details. Success in the public hospitality business hinges on details.

The following questions represent a checklist that should assist in the planning of a service system:

- How will customers arrive? As pairs, singles, or large groups? This will determine the size of your bar, and the types of seating you will install.

- Will customers arrive by car? If so, do you have adequate, safe parking available?

- Where will customers enter and how will they be greeted? By whom? When? Where?

- Will you use the lounge to accommodate customers waiting to be seated in the dining room?

- Where will your lounge be located in relation to the entrance and to the dining room?

- Who will take the customer's drink orders, a cocktail waitress or the bartender?

- How will you call waiting customers when their dining room table is ready?

- Will the lounge check be transferred to the dining room, or must customers pay before leaving?

- How will your lounge be subdivided into stations to assure prompt service?

- Will your lounge have smoking and nonsmoking areas? How large will each area be?

- Will your lounge staff wear uniforms or costumes?

- How will the drink orders be delivered to the bartender? Electronically? Verbally? Written?

- How will servers know when their drink orders are ready to be picked up?

- Will cocktail servers garnish their own drinks?

- What will your policies be for doubles and extra strong drinks? Will you limit the size or number?

- Who will approve mistakes and voided check items?

- Who will handle any complaints that might arise?

- How will the checks be presented to the customer?

- Who will cashier the check?

- Where will charge card sales be written up?

- Will there be a coatroom? Free? Coin operated? Coat checks?

- Where will restrooms be located?

- Where will telephone and cigarette machines be located?

Glassware

Some establishments use a wide variety of glasses in their bars, while others use a very limited selection of glassware. On occasion you may find a bar that uses only one glass for all the drinks they serve. The "one glass fits all" practice is questionable, however, because of its lack of universal appeal. Some glassware has an elegant appearance appropriate for certain settings. Other glassware suggests bargain prices or fun and fits well with the desired marketing message of a business.

Selecting Glassware

Below are important factors by which to select glassware:

- Style
- Size
- Strength
- Usefulness
- Cost

The style should be based on your desired image and your customers expectations. It should be easy to clean, stackable (if that is a desired feature), and in tune with the overall decor and atmosphere of your bar.

Glass sizes should be appropriate for the quantity of liquor you wish to pour into drinks, and that, of course, will be related to the prices you plan to charge. Simply put, you don't need an eight ounce glass if you are dispensing three ounces of beverage (even with ice).

The strength of a glass is important in liquor operations. Bar glasses are handled much more than most pieces of dining room ware. The speed with which they are handled and washed makes them extra vulnerable to chipping and cracking. Select stock made especially for the hotel and restaurant trade, it will save you money over the long run.

The usefulness of glassware is something only you can determine. Don't buy glasses that are made for items you do not serve. For example, most pubs do not need champagne glasses.

Try to achieve consistency in your selection of glassware. Don't mix fancy with plain, extra large with small, or clear with colored glassware. The average price of standard bar glassware is about $15 a dozen depending on size and style.

How Much Should You Buy?

This will depend upon the estimated volume of sales for the various drinks you serve. You will most likely sell more martinis and manhattans than liqueurs in a dinner restaurant. Therefore, you would need more cocktail and rocks glasses than cordial glasses.

Keep in mind that some glasses will be in use on tables, while others will be soiled and waiting to be washed behind the bar. You should have a large enough supply of glasses to handle all contingencies. Most establishments will keep a reserve stock in the back-of-the-house to be used for replacements and very busy occasions. You should plan on breakage of 25% or more per year. Once a glass is chipped, no matter how slightly, it must be removed from service.

The example in Figure 5.6 is for illustrative purposes only, the actual amount of glassware you will need will vary according to your type of establishment, the drinks you serve and the sales of each type, the seating capacity, whether or not you cater large functions, and your glasswashing capabilities.

Figure 5.6:

Sample Bar Inventory

Type of Glass	Quantity
5 oz. Rocks	13 dozen
5 oz. Highball	12 dozen
10 oz. Collins	12 dozen
4 oz. Sour	6 dozen
4 oz. Cocktail	13 dozen
5 oz. Brandy Snifter	2 dozen
12 oz. Beer	13 dozen
6 oz. Wine	12 dozen
2 oz. Sherry	3 dozen
4 oz. Champagne	3 dozen
1 oz. Cordial	3 dozen

Food Service in the Lounge

Whether to serve food in a bar is a question every operator must decide. In some states food service is required for certain kinds of licenses. Some patrons enjoy eating at a bar, but others resent people eating beside them when they are drinking at a bar. Your decision depends on the wants and needs of your targeted clientele.

Serving food at a bar impacts on a number of operational issues, such as flow of traffic, ambiance, and seat turnover. The following questions must be answered.

- What will be on the menu at the bar?
- Where will the food be prepared?
- Who will prepare it?
- When will it be prepared?
- What equipment will be needed to prepare and hold it?
- Who will deliver the food order to the customer?
- Who will cashier the check?
- Who will bus the tables?

Snacks and casual food are good business builders for a bar, but be aware that the overall cleanliness of a bar can be impacted if provision is not made for regularly scheduled cleanings. Some products, such as peanuts and popcorn, are very popular, but messy. If a regular program of table and floor care is observed, these snacks will not present a problem.

Environment and Decor

Everything a customer sees, feels, smells, or hears in your establishment is a part of its decor. The instant customers pull on your front door handle, they are experiencing your decor. A massive front door with heavy duty hardware conveys one image, while a small, lightweight front door with economical hardware conveys a totally different image.

So it is with everything in your establishment; colors, sizes, shapes, weights, and textures are all part of your decorating scheme and must be coordinated to produce the image you desire.

Who Should Decorate?

You can do it yourself, or you can hire an interior decorator. There are dangers in doing it yourself, however, even if you have the talent. The main problem is that decorating is a time-consuming and all encompassing task. As a manager or owner, your time is too valuable to get tied down to one activity for too long. Other parts of your business may suffer and erase any saving from doing your own decorating. Another danger is, you may lack knowledge of the most up-to-date materials and techniques that a professional decorator would know about.

Utilizing a professional decorator with whom you work closely is the ideal situation. The owner may have a concept in mind, in which case the role of the decorator is to design around that concept in the best way possible. Or, the owner may commission a decorator to create an original design, transferring a broad range of responsibility for all aspects of the project.

In both instances the close working relationship is important. In the first instance, the owner must communicate clearly and completely the objectives. To the extent that this is not done, the decorator's ideas rather than the owner's will dominate. In the second instance, it is imperative that the decorator know the monetary limitations of the project. Much time, money, and effort can be wasted if the financial parameters are not established at the onset of the project.

A Clear Message

Your customers should never be in doubt as to what your message is. Everything about your establishment should contribute to your desired image, including:

- Name of the business
- Building design
- Signs (colors, size, type of print)
- Tables and chairs
- Chinaware and flatware
- Tablecloths and napkins
- Carpeting or flooring
- Wall hangings and drapes

- Light fixtures
- Menus (the physical menu)
- Floor plan (table spacing)
- Uniforms
- Plants or other decorator objects

In addition to the above, plan carefully for safety, sanitation, sound control, and atmospheric comfort (heating, ventilation, air conditioning). Lighting is also important. Coordinate the intensity and color of your lighting along with your fixture styles. Consider all the uses of light— background effect, accent, and safety in lighting walkways or directing people.

Basic Design Principles

The wants and needs of your targeted clientele should dictate the type and style of decor. You must develop a theme or concept for your bar and maintain it through every aspect of the atmosphere and decor as well as the food and beverage offerings. Only then are you ready to begin selecting your furniture, fixtures, and appointments.

Below are principles of design to keep in mind as you plan your decor.

Balance. Balance is the quality that gives a room a pleasing sense of togetherness. However, balance will vary as a result of the number of people using the area, so it is important to consider the average occupancy. A crowded bar decorated with dark colors and low lighting may look heavy and imbalanced if it has not been properly decorated.

Emphasis. Emphasis refers to the focal point or center of interest in a room. There should not be more than one focal point or emphasis in a room. But, the use of walls, partitions, and folding doors in a bar could allow for several different focal points in the same overall space. For instance, in one room the band could be the focal point, while in an adjacent area, the giant TV screen could be the focal point. Emphasis can also be achieved through the positioning of furniture or contrasts in color, texture, and size and shape. The same tactics used for emphasis can also draw attention away from an unattractive aspect of a room.

Flow. Flow encourages the natural and free movement of the eye from one area to another and can be accomplished through repetition, and progression of sizes. In a bar, the strategic hanging of paintings or artifacts related to your theme on the walls will create flow.

Proportion. Proportion refers to the relationship of one object to another. For example, a large, imposing bar in a small room would appear overwhelming and out of proportion.

Colors

The next step is to determine your color scheme. Psychological experiments have shown that color can affect the mood and behavior of people. Warm colors would be most effective in an informal, lively establishment. Cool colors are better suited to more formal, relaxed places. Warm neutral colors are often the most appropriate background for bars catering to a more diverse group. Three families of colors lend themselves well to bars: Greens, which are friendly in mood and mix well with other colors; browns, which are warm, comfortable, and easy to work with; and reds, which are stimulating and useful as accents.

Floor and Wall Coverings. Selections of fabrics, floors, and wall coverings are also important to the atmosphere of a bar. These items must be chosen with forethought. Consider the type of image you want to convey, as well as upkeep and durability. Synthetic fibers and materials are easily maintained. The most common floor coverings are wood, carpeting, brick, stone, and ceramic or vinyl tile.

Wall coverings may be rigid, such as plaster, brick, and wallboard; or flexible, such as paper and cloth. Vinyl-treated papers are well suited for a bar or lounge since they are washable and can be very decorative.

Furniture. Be it classic, contemporary, or modern, the furniture, along with other appointments, is going to play a major role. As always, it is necessary to analyze your clientele, and the reasons they come to your bar.

A lounge with live entertainment and dancing needs quite different furnishings than a quiet, conversational type bar. Where there is dancing, there will be less room (and probably less need) for large, comfortable pieces of furniture. Many people will be mingling or dancing, thereby necessitating less area for sitting and more area for movement. On the other hand a place that is trying to convey an image of intimacy should have plenty of tables, comfortable chairs, and cozy booths. The style and arrangement of furniture serves to reinforce the image of a bar.

Lighting

Poor or inappropriate lighting can destroy the whole effect of a bar. The color of your lighting plays an important role in creating the image you desire. White light, for instance, shows colors as they really are, but does not add charm. Cool color lights, such as blue, give a feeling of more space to the room, but add a chilling effect. Warm color lights, on the other hand, can soften the chilling effect by dulling the cool colors.

The position of lights is also important. Light sources that are located below eye level will tend to make a place seem more intimate and friendly. The higher the source of light, the more formal is the effect rendered. Small direct lights will emphasize a focal point, large diffused ones tend to unify a space.

Troubleshooting Tips. There are an infinite number of possibilities for decorating and creating atmosphere in a bar. The best approach is to narrow down the choices by carefully defining your concept, and desired clientele, and then using professional decorators. Unless you have particularly strong skills in this area, your time will be better spent on other planning or managerial responsibilities. Figure 5.7 (pp. 66-67) will help you focus on important issues of atmosphere and decor.

Figure 5.7:

Tips for Improving the Atmosphere of a Bar

Problem	Negative Effect	Suggested Improvements
Faded, drab, or dirty looking colors	Causes dull, listless feeling on part of customers.	Use new paint, murals, hanging plants
Damaged chairs and tables	Gives guests the impression your establishment is unsuccessful.	Refinish or replace chairs and tables.
Bright room	Lacks coziness of a friendly lounge.	Adjust rheostats. Re-paint walls with intimate colors. Soften walls with accents. Replace light fixtures if necessary.
Large room	Creates feeling of being lost in a crowd.	Group tables to give impression of intimacy. Use divider walls, planters, and screens to break up the huge room look.
Ceilings too high	Causes heat loss, increases noise levels, and makes room seem impersonal.	Lower the ceiling, or install sections of false ceiling. Hang interesting objects.
Overcrowded feeling	May cause restlessness or irritation at being bumped accidentally or constantly having to move for someone to pass.	Rearrange existing tables and, if possible, use an adjacent room for overflow seating.

Problem	Negative Effect	Suggested Improvements
No variety in presentation of drinks	Diminishes customers desire to reorder	Change liquor list more often. Highlight different drinks. Set up attractive wine displays to stimulate interest. Feature holiday and seasonal drinks.
Standing customers crowded around tables or booths	Disrupts atmosphere. Gives guests feeling of being intruded upon.	Contain by rope cordon or dividers or portable screens.
Overheated lounge	Causes drowsiness and irritation.	Lower the thermostat, improve ventilation, but avoid drafts in larger rooms.
Moody or impatient employees	Bad moods are evident to guests and may cause irritation, and dislike of the establishment.	Identify problems and strive for a positive work environment.
Untidy appearance and unprofessional attitudes on part of staff	Apprehension on part of guests	Supervise the activities of the lounge more closely. Conduct training sessions to improve attitude. Install a dress code, or buy new uniforms to improve appearance. Be more selective when hiring.
Employees favoring certain customers	May cause irritation to others due to delays in serving.	Discuss at training sessions.

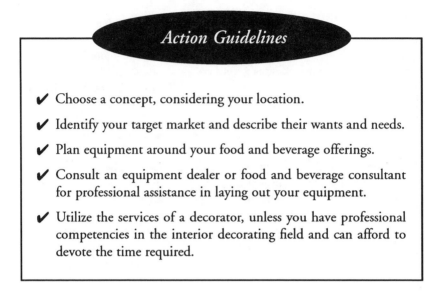

Action Guidelines

✔ Choose a concept, considering your location.

✔ Identify your target market and describe their wants and needs.

✔ Plan equipment around your food and beverage offerings.

✔ Consult an equipment dealer or food and beverage consultant for professional assistance in laying out your equipment.

✔ Utilize the services of a decorator, unless you have professional competencies in the interior decorating field and can afford to devote the time required.

OPERATING PROFITABLY

To operate a bar profitably, one must keep a tight control over all *profit centers*. A profit center is a segment of the overall operation, an activity, that can increase or decrease profits. Typically, there are seven profit centers in a beverage establishment. If a bar also sells food, it would have two additional profit centers—menu planning and food preparation.

1. Purchasing
2. Receiving
3. Storing
4. Issuing
5. Production
6. Service
7. Cashiering

Purchasing the right products in the proper quantities for your bar is important. Of equal importance is secured storage and proper use. Liquor is a tempting product that should not be left sitting about the premises. It should be stored and logged into an inventory book as soon as received. When a bottle is issued, the withdrawal should be recorded in the inventory book. Standard drink recipes should be used by all bartenders to insure a consistent taste and liquor content for all drinks. Finally, to close the control loop, all monies collected should be accounted for.

Inventory Turnover Rate

It is said, in the food and beverage business, that it takes about ten dollars of additional sales to make up for every dollar lost through poor purchasing. Like any retail enterprise, a bar cannot afford to carry dead stock. Money tied up on storeroom shelves gathers dust, not interest.

In certain instances, such as when fine wines and exotic drinks are featured on the menu, a bar may intentionally carry a number of slow-moving items in stock for merchandising reasons. Nevertheless, a manager can exercise a high degree of inventory control by calculating a turnover rate for the other 80 percent of the stock.

Your *inventory turnover rate* is the number of times your inventory is turned into cash, within a given period of time. Put another way, it measures how long it takes to sell the goods you buy. The method for calculating an inventory turnover rate is shown in the following example:

Step 1: Calculate the cost of the beverages consumed.

Beginning Beverage Inventory 1/1/94	$3,000
Plus: Beverage Purchases 1/1—1/31	9,000
Total	$12,000
Less: Ending Beverage Inventory 1/31/94	2,800
Cost of Beverages Consumed	$ 9,200

Step 2: Calculate the average beverage inventory.

Beginning Beverage Inventory 1/1/94	$3,000
Plus: Ending Beverage Inventory 1/31/94	2,800
	$5,800

$$\frac{\$5,800}{2} = \$2,900 \text{ Average Beverage Inventory}$$

Step 3: Calculate the inventory turnover rate.

$$\frac{\text{Cost of Beverages Consumed}}{\text{Average Inventory}} = \text{Inventory Turnover Rate}$$

$$\frac{\$9,200}{\$2,900} = 3.17 \text{ times a month}$$

In the preceding example, the beverage inventory was turned over about three times a month or about every nine and half days. Turnover rates may vary by season. The optimum turnover rate is the highest number of times that covers your operations adequately between reorders, along with a small safety margin for unexpected increases in business.

It is recommended that all bars keep some sort of written record of items ordered from distributors, and compare shipments with purchase orders. The receiver can then quickly spot substitutions or incorrect items. This procedure prevents controversy about orders and deliveries and serves as part of an audit trail for cost control. The first documentation is the purchase order (see Figure 6.1, p. 72).

Your Initial Inventory

Three categories of spirits are carried in most bars—bar brands, call brands and premium liquors—distinguished by cost and quality. Bar brands, also called well brands, are the least costly liquors, and are used when a customer does not request a particular brand. Accordingly, drinks made with bar brands are priced somewhat lower. Call brands are those liquors that people ask for by name, and premium brands are the top shelf items that customers request by name.

It is not possible or feasible for a bar to carry every product available. But it is essential for a bar to carry a reasonable variety of liquors in order for customers to have a choice. For example, there are literally hundreds of Scotch whiskeys produced. Yet, a bar could have a good representation of the various types and quality ranges with only eight to twelve brands on its shelves. Other types of liquors do not require that many brands be stocked in order to offer a good representation of the product. Ideally, if a bar does not carry the specific brand a customer may request, the bartender should be able to offer an acceptable substitute to a customer.

The quantities of each brand to be ordered for your initial inventory will depend on the wants and needs of your clientele. Liquor sales representatives will be eager to help you get started. A good salesperson, who wants your continued business, will not overload you.

When selecting distributors, your focus should be on the popularity of their brands, their terms of payment and discounts, promotional assistance, the availability of free wine lists, and their frequency of deliveries.

In evaluating brand popularity, distinguish real demand from artificial demand. You should observe whether the requests for a product you don't carry are coming from a few people or many. On occasion, an overzealous

DATE				No. 1185
	The Ticker Tape Bar & Grill			

The Ticker Tape Bar & Grill
PURCHASE ORDER
Please furnish the following—All carriers charges prepaid

Qty.	Unit	Description	Unit Price	Amount

Received by_____   Purchasing Agent_____

INVOICE MUST ACCOMPANY MERCHANDISE

Figure 6.1: Sample Purchase Order.

salesperson has been known to have friends patronize a newly opened establishment and repeatedly order the product the salesperson is trying to sell to the bar, in order to create what seems to be a large demand for it.

Maximum and minimum inventory levels should be established for all items, based on their actual sales history, and should be adhered to. There is little point in buying several cases of a slow moving product to obtain a discount of a few dollars, if an alternative use of the money would yield an equal or greater return.

How to Select Your Inventory

The most important consideration when selecting inventory is your clientele. Who are they? What will they expect when they patronize your establishment? When will they arrive—in the daytime or at night? What is their purpose—business lunch, entertainment, after-work relaxation? The answers to these questions will indicate the types of drinks your guests will tend to order.

It is not unreasonable to limit your stock of certain beverages and suggest an alternate brand. The goal of inventory management is to carry the brands that are needed to keep your customers happy, while not tying up your money needlessly. Occasionally, some premium brands are carried mainly for prestige value and as long as it's not overdone, that practice is acceptable. Following is a list of the alcoholic beverages carried by most full service bars.

- Scotch whiskies
- Canadian whiskies
- Blended whiskies
- Gins
- Brandies
- Fruit Flavored Brandies
- Beers and Ales
- Irish whiskies
- Bourbon whiskies
- Vodkas
- Tequilas
- Cognacs
- Liqueurs & Cordials
- Wines

The reason bars carry three levels of liquors—bar brands, call brands, and premium brands—is to provide a choice for all tastes and all pocketbooks. Bar brands are very acceptable products but usually have little or no customer recognition. In some establishments, drinks made with bar brands constitute the bulk of the sales volume.

In addition to your spirits, you will need to carry an adequate inventory of wines and beers. The optimum size of a wine inventory will vary according to the bar's clientele and type of food served.

Beers are usually carried in bottle or keg form. The selection of brands is heavily influenced by regional preferences. However, if your bar caters to tourists and traveling business people, your decisions might need to include national preferences. At least one dark beer should be carried in restaurant bars, and one or more light beers are recommended for diet conscious people. Today, most bars will also carry two or more nonalcoholic beers.

Figure 6.2 is a sampling of what you should consider carrying. The amount of backup stock carried in a liquor storeroom or wine cellar will depend on several factors:

- Frequency of deliveries
- Storage space available
- Availability of certain products
- Budget for liquor inventories

Know Your Metrics

The liquor industry has switched to the metric system. This makes little difference to the average customer because a 750 milliliter bottle looks like a fifth and a liter looks like a quart, but a bar manager should know the difference. Here is how the old and new sizes compare:

Old Sizes	*New Sizes*
Miniature—1.6 oz.	50 ml.—1.7 oz.
Half pint—8 oz.	200 ml.—6.8 oz.
Pint—16 oz.	500 ml.—16.9 oz.
Fifth—25.6 oz.	750 ml.—25.4 oz.
Quart—32 oz.	1 Liter—33.8 oz.
Half Gallon—64 oz.	1.75 Liter—59.2 oz.

It is very important for inventory control purposes to select the proper sizes for your bar operation and to stick with those sizes. Mixing of sizes can lead to inaccurate valuation of stock when extending inventory totals. Most bars prefer to buy liters and 750 ml., because the bottles fit into speed racks and are easier for bartenders to handle.

Receiving, Storing, and Issuing Liquor

All alcoholic beverages should be checked in and put away in a secure storage room immediately after deliveries are received. The receiver should check to make sure that the proper brands and bottle sizes were delivered. Cases should be opened, counted and checked for breakage

The Ticker Tape Bar & Grill _all 750 ml unless otherwise stated_					
Item	**Quantity on Hand**			**Unit Cost**	**Value**
	Storeroom	Bar	Total		
BOURBON					
Beam's Choice					
Old Grand Dad					
Wild Turkey					
TENNESSEE WHISKEY					
Jack Daniels No. 7					
Jack Daniels No. 7 Green					
BLENDED WHISKEY					
Fleischmann's Preferred					
Seagrams 7 Crown					
SCOTCH					
King William IV					
Chivas Regal					
Cutty Sark					
RUM					
Bacardi 151 Proof					
Mr. Boston Light Rum					
Bacardi Amber Label					
Myers Original Dark					
Mount Gay Eclipse					
BRANDY & COGNAC					
St. Charles Brandy					
Courvoisier VS Cognac					
Hennessy VS Cognac					
FLAVORED BRANDY					
Leroux Apricot Brandy					
Arrow Blackberry Brandy					
Jacquin Peach Brandy					
GRAND TOTAL INVENTORY					

Figure 6.2: Sample Liquor Inventory Sheet. Note: _The use of product names is for illustrative purposes and is not intended as a recommendation nor is the list of liquors comprehensive._

The Ticker Tape Bar & Grill

RECEIVER'S REPORT

No. _____
Date _____
Received by _____

Purveyor	Qty.	Unit Size	Description	√	Unit Price	Amount	Total Amount	Distribution	
								Direct to Bar	To Liquor Storeroom

Figure 6.3: Receiver's Report used to record all incoming shipments of wines, spirits, beer, and bar supplies. All items received, including promotional items and gifts must be recorded.

before the delivery slip is signed by the receiver. Only competent employees of legal age should be allowed to receive and handle alcoholic beverages. Figure 6.3 shows a sample form for confirming shipments.

On occasion, a delivery may arrive without the appropriate delivery slip. In such an event, Merchandise Received without Bill form (Figure 6.4,), should be filled out with a description of the merchandise received and the signatures of the delivery truck driver and the receiver. This form confirms that the goods that were actually received and avoids the possibility of confusion at a later date.

If incorrect merchandise has to be returned, have the truck driver sign a Request for Credit Memo (Figure 6.5, p. 78) when you relinquish the goods. In the past, when such documentation was written by hand, it was possible to simply erase a returned item from a delivery slip and retotal it. Today, with computerized billing, it does no good to simply change a bill, the data must be entered into the computer. The Request for Credit Memo is proof that an incorrect item was indeed returned for credit. It also serves as a reminder to the accounting department to make sure the credit comes through at the end of the month.

B11860

The Ticker Tape Bar & Grill
MERCHANDISE RECEIVED WITHOUT BILL
Please send us a bill for the following items

From: _____   Date:_____

_____

Quantity	Item	Amount	
		Total	
Delivery Driver: _____		By: _____	

Figure 6.4: Merchandise Received Without Bill form used to verify items received without a delivery slip.

```
                                                        B11860
                    The Ticker Tape Bar & Grill
                  REQUEST FOR CREDIT MEMO
                Please send us a credit memo for the following
         To: _____    Date:_____

             _____


         Quantity            Item                       Amount
         _____
         _____
         _____
         _____
         _____

                                            Total _____

         Delivery Driver: _____   By: _____
```

Figure 6.5: Request for Credit Memos stipulate the reason for a return of merchandise and serve as a follow-up reminder to check on credits.

A liquor storeroom should be well-lighted, ventilated, and dry. It should have a secure door lock, and keys should be issued to only one or two people who have a need to access it. Storeroom shelves should be spaced well enough apart to accommodate the tallest bottles, standing up. The uppermost shelf should be easily reachable.

Every product should have a specific storage location on the storeroom shelves that corresponds to its position on the inventory sheet. This significantly reduces the time required to take inventory.

A record should be kept of all withdrawals from the storeroom. One method is a Bar Requisition form (Figure 6.6). At the end of each shift, a bartender gathers all the empty liquor bottles at the bar and fills out a requisition form for replacements. The requisition slip is turned in to the storeroom, and the bartender receives a bottle for bottle exchange for the same brand and size. This procedure not only controls the storeroom but also keeps the *par stock* at the bar at the desired level. The term par stock refers to the total number of bottles that should always be present at the

```
┌─────────────────────────────────────────────────────┐
│              The Ticker Tape Bar & Grill             │
│              BAR REQUISITION                         │
│                     Date: _____, 19___      │
│ _____ Department  │
├─────────────────────────────────────────────────────┤
│ Issued to the undersigned.                           │
│ _____ │
│ _____ │
│ _____ │
│ _____ │
│ _____ │
│ _____ │
│ _____ │
│                                                      │
│ No. 1234              Signed _____  │
│                       Department _____  │
└─────────────────────────────────────────────────────┘
```

Figure 6.6: Bar Requisition forms should be used when restocking a bar. They provide a record of items that are issued out of the storeroom.

bar. It is usually the number of bottles required for a day's business, without having to restock. In some very busy bars, with limited space, restocking must be done at the start of each shift.

Your Beverage Sales Representatives

In noncontrol states, liquors, wines, and beers are sold by private business enterprises in the same manner that food products are sold. Their salespeople usually call on bars on a weekly or biweekly basis. Since no one distributor carries all brands, it is normal to buy from several distributors. You should arrange for salespeople to call on you at a mutually convenient time.

Salespeople can be valuable sources of information on the local popularity of the various types of beverages. They can also help you plan an opening inventory. With their help, you can keep current on price increases, product shortages, new products, special promotions, mer-

The Ticker Tape Bar & Grill
STOCK RECORD CARD

Item:_____

Purveyor:_____

Max:_____   Article:_____ Size:_____   Unit Cost:_____

Min:_____   Location:_____   Unit:_____   Cost per Oz.:_____

Date	In	Out	Bal.	Date	In	Out	Bal.	Date	In	Out	Bal.

Figure 6.7: Stock Record Card is another method for recording inventory activity in the stock room.

chandising aids, and special discounts. When evaluating the services of a distributor, consider the following questions:

- Does the distributor offer adequate delivery service?
- Does it require minimum orders?
- Will it split cases?
- Does it have to substitute products frequently due to being out of stock?
- What types of discounts does it offer?
- Does it supply sales promotional material?

Let salespeople know what your philosophy is on inventory turnover so that they can work with you. Also, let them know what your marketing concept is— for instance, do you want to be able to make every conceivable drink or just the popular drinks? The better you communicate with salespeople, the better they will know what you want, and the better they will be able to serve you.

Finally, realize that salespeople are just like all other people. There are some very good ones and some not so good ones. When you have a choice between distributors, focus on the dependability and willingness of salespeople to help you as you get started.

Using Standardized Drink Recipes

Customers want a consistent drink every time they order. Variations in taste, size, and type of glass among bartenders are not infrequent occurrences in some bars. These inconsistencies may occur from drink to drink, or from bartender to bartender. You can avoid this problem by standardizing the recipes of all your drinks. The main advantages of using standardized drink recipes are:

- They assure high quality drinks all day, every day.
- They are useful when training new bartenders.
- They reduce overpouring.
- They allow a more accurate accounting of bar sales.

A standardized recipe is a set of instructions that tells your bartender what your house policy is in regard to the type of glassware to be used, the quantity and type of ingredients, and the method of preparation. The success of standardized drink recipes is based on using specific products and portion sizes. An example of a standardized recipe is the following:

File cards make excellent drink recipe cards. Every bar should have an easily accessible set, stored safely in a metal file box. The advantage file cards have over recipe books is additions can be made easily, without upsetting the alphabetical arrangement. They may be transferred to drink costing sheets. Recipes that you may develop, to be featured as house drinks, should be carefully tested before being served to customers.

Martini Recipe

7 oz. Rock glass/fill with ice cubes
2 oz. gin
1/2 oz. dry Vermouth
Stir and serve with a sip stick and olive or twist

Overpouring is Expensive

If a bar uses standard drink recipes and trains its employees well, it should not have a serious problem of overpouring. Many bars, however, do not and consequently, many bartenders do as they please—some overpour thinking they will get bigger tips from customers.

Overpouring is a very costly practice that should be eliminated. The following example illustrates just how expensive it can be, even when only a small amount is overpoured in each drink.

That $11,498 should be in the bottom line of your income statement. When a bartender overpours, your profits are being given away, and you are not even getting credit for the gift. The greater concern, of course, is that unless the practice is stopped, larger amounts may be overpoured in the future.

Some bars take overpouring so seriously, they give a pouring test to their bartenders every two weeks. If bartenders fail a test, they are given one week to regain their pouring accuracy. If they fail the second time, they are dismissed.

Assume the following:

a) A bartender overpours 1/4 oz. of liquor in every drink.

b) Your bar volume is about $1,200 a day.

c) Drink prices average $3 a drink.

d) The average cost of a 750 ml. bottle of liquor is $8.

Calculation:

About 400 drinks are sold daily ($1,200 ÷ $3 = 400 drinks)

400 drinks x 1/4 oz. = 100 oz. lost daily due to overpouring.

100 oz. = 3.93 bottles (750 ml. bottles contain 25.4 oz.)

3.93 bottles x $8.00 (avg. cost of bottle) = $31.50 lost daily

$31.50 x 365 days = $11,498 annual cost of overpouring

The Importance of Supervision

It is easy to not look for problems when things appear to be going well. For that reason, some bar owners lose sizable sums of money each year, without realizing it is happening. This type of operator may never know just how great the business might have been, had better control been maintained over it. Profit leaks can occur from mistakes, waste, and dishonest practices. To plug the leaks, control procedures should be installed in all profit centers and close supervision should be maintained to insure that the procedures are being carried out.

Following is a list of 34 situations that can cause a bar to lose profits, but are correctable.

1. Not keeping the liquor room locked and taking other precautions to prevent theft and misuse

2. Not safeguarding the keys to the liquor storeroom by issuing them to only one or two supervisory persons whose duties require access to the storeroom

3. Not following up on credits for merchandise backordered or returned because of damage

4. Excessive buying; carrying too much stock in relation to sales volume, tying up working capital that could be used for other investment opportunities

5. Not taking advantage of discounts and promotional deals, which amounts to overpaying for bar stock

6. Not checking invoices and payments against receiving records to detect any shortages, backorders and incorrect prices

7. Not buying liquors in consistent bottle sizes (750 ml or 1 liters), and consequently applying incorrect values when taking inventory

8. Failure to accurately record additions to and subtractions from inventory in a perpetual inventory book or on bin cards

9. Excessive breakage due to mishandling of products and not having a management person verify breakage when it occurs

10. Not making spot checks made of the par stock at the bar, to assure that the total bottle count (full, partially full, and empty bottles) is what it should be

11. Not taking a complete physical inventory at frequent intervals to calculate the pouring cost percentage and to verify the accuracy of the perpetual inventory figures

12. Allowing products to spoil due to improper storage conditions, such as moisture, excessive heat or cold, and exposure to intense light for long periods of time

13. Failure to take corrective action quickly when the cause of a problem is discovered

14. Failure to properly orient and train new employees

15. Not assigning clear responsibility for control of the liquor supply to one management person

16. Not using a system of forced issues to get rid of dead stock or very slow moving items when cash flow needs improvement

17. Bartenders not adhering to standard recipes and overpouring liquors

18. Drinks not properly priced, to yield the desired pouring cost percentage

19. Bartenders unorganized and too slow to capitalize on rush hour potential

20. Bartenders drinking stock and giving free drinks to other employees and friends

21. Theft of products by employees and delivery people who enter the establishment

22. Bartenders not using standard glassware for drinks

23. Bartenders trying to run a mental tab instead of collecting for each drink as served, then collecting improper amounts

24. Not providing standard measuring tools for bartenders to use, or bartenders failing to use these tools when mixing drinks

25. No standard house policies established by management and explained to all bar personnel

26. Garnishes allowed to spoil by not covering and refrigerating them overnight

27. No daily record kept of drinks sold to compare with the quantity of liquor consumed that day

28. Carelessness at bar resulting in excessive spillage and breakage

29. Overstaffing, by scheduling extra bartenders and waitpeople when not needed

30. Not keeping adequate sales records to track customer preference trends

31. Making wine and liquor lists so complicated they confuse customers and dampen sales

32. Failure to advertise special promotions and events to the extent allowed by law

33. Failure to meet customers' wants and needs, in regard to the liquors offered and the atmosphere of the establishment

34. Failure to gather feedback from customers and assess how pleased they are with the establishment

Dishonest Practices

Observers of the retail industry indicate pilferage is a major problem and acknowledge that employees represent a significant segment of the pilferers. The retail beverage industry is no exception. Products or services can be given away, overcharged or undercharged for, or charged for but not recorded. The list of possibilities is lengthy. How then can management deal with the problem? The answer is to hire the best employees possible, maintain tight controls, and supervise closely.

It has been said that 25 percent of all people are completely honest (see Figure 6.8). Because of their beliefs or moral fiber, they are not interested in self-gain by committing dishonest acts, and they resent people who are so inclined. Another 25 percent are to varying degrees, attracted by or constantly in search of dishonest opportunities. The remaining fifty percent of people fall somewhere in the middle. They are basically honest, but if constantly tempted, some may be swayed toward the dishonest end of the spectrum.

Tendencies		
25% Extremely Honest	50% Neutral	25% Have Dishonest Tendencies (to varying degrees)

Figure 6.8: Honesty of Employees.

Obviously, the object of a good security program is to sway the neutral group toward the honest end of the spectrum. Tactics include removing temptations, controlling products and sales, setting policies and standards for conduct, and letting people know their actions are being observed. These are important deterrents to dishonest practices, however, the first line of defense is to interview applicants thoroughly and check references, which is discussed in Chapter 7.

Entertainment

Entertainment is often a business builder. Good entertainment can attract new customers and keep your existing customers from drifting to competitors. A common misconception, however, is that entertainment will automatically improve business volume. To the contrary, ineffective entertainment can be a financial drain on your business. Not all entertainment is good, and cost is not an assurance of quality or results. When considering adding entertainment, you should ask yourself the following questions:

- What type of entertainment best fits your format?
- Do you have excess seating capacity? Can you accommodate additional volume with your present facilities?
- Are your competitors using entertainment successfully? If so, what kind?
- Are your customers asking for a certain type of entertainment, or in the case of a new bar, will your target market expect it?

Three types of entertainment may be considered for a bar—individual performers, bands, and mechanical background music. Mechanical background music includes jukeboxes and tape systems. It is the least expensive type of entertainment, and in case of a jukebox, can be an income producer. It should be noted, however, that if a jukebox's selections or the volume at which it is played are not pleasing to your clientele, you may lose customers.

Individual performers, such as piano and guitar players, are the next least expensive. If they are good, they can add a uniquely pleasant quality to a barroom. Some performers, with a loyal following, are capable of attracting their fans wherever they work. Their popularity in bars emanates largely from their personalities and their ability to relate to audiences. It is important to audition this type of performer carefully before hiring. The range of talent on the market is broad, and a poor choice of entertainer could actually have a negative effect on business.

Bands can be good attractions if they are popular. But, the more popular they are, the more expensive they are. In general, they are more feasible for establishments that have a large seating capacity and a price structure that can absorb the band's high cost. Bands also require setup space, and numerous electrical outlets.

When dancing is instituted, entertainment must be monitored very carefully because while people are dancing they are not eating or drinking. Cover charges can offset the cost of entertainment, with the caution that the clientele must perceive the entertainment to be worth the price of admission.

Another consideration is the size of your dance floor. Too small a floor discourages your patrons from dancing, and too large a floor wastes valuable sales-generating seating space.

Entertainment should be evaluated regularly. Ask the following questions:

- Is entertainment increasing sales?
- Is it attracting the type of clientele you seek?
- Are profits increasing as a result of entertainment?

An analysis sheet for evaluating entertainment is shown in Figure 6.9 (p. 88). It can serve as a useful measure to compare the results entertainers achieve and to suggest when corrective action is warranted.

It is important to know your clientele—who they are, what they expect, and how they think. For many smaller bars, mechanical background music supplied by a jukebox or a leased music system is perfect. Music can set the mood of your bar, and a wide variety is available—intimate mood music, melodic light classical music, top forty pop music, and heavy-metal rock music, to name but a few. In any case, your choice should be based on what your target market wants.

Your Break-Even Point for Entertainment

Assume you have excess capacity. That is, on certain nights of the week you have many empty seats. This concerns you because your overhead costs go on whether you have a half-filled house or a full house.

Weekly Entertainment Analysis Sheet

Week of ___	Name of Entertainer	1 = Total Revenue	2 + Food Sales	3 Beverage Sales	4 Total Cost of Entertainment	= 5 Cost of Entertainment	+ 6 Advertising and any other Costs	+ 7 Ratio (%) Entertainment Cost to Food and Beverage Sales (4/1=7)

Figure 6.9: This form is used to summarize information and analyze results of various entertainers and allow comparisons to be made.

Consequently, you could significantly increase your business volume without incurring any additional overhead costs. To attract more people to your bar on those slow nights, you decide to offer entertainment and hire a four-piece band. You run an advertisement in the local newspaper to let the community know you have entertainment.

Your main concern at this point is that the entertainment, at the very least, must pay its own way—break even. If it does not do that, it will not have accomplished its purpose of increasing business, and is in fact, a further drain on profits and must be changed or terminated.

The following example, which assumes you operate with a 20 percent pouring cost, illustrates how you can calculate a break-even point for the entertainment:

Step 1: Determine the total cost of the entertainment.

Cost of entertainment ($600 per night for 3 nights) =	$1,800
Cost of advertisement	200
Total Cost Related to the Entertainment	$2,000

Step 2: Establish your contribution margin.
Formula:
100% - Pouring Cost Percentage (PC) = Contribution Margin
100% - 20% = 80% (contribution margin)

Step 3: Calculate your break-even point.
Formula:
Total Cost of Entertainment ÷ Contribution Margin = Break-Even Point
$2,000 ÷ .80 = $2,500
$2,500 = Break-Even Point

It is important to note that the break-even point is the amount of *additional* sales that must be obtained. In this example you will rely on increased sales volume to carry the entertainment cost and will not need to change your drink prices. If sales increase by $2,500, the bar will have taken in just enough to cover the liquor cost for additional drinks and pay for the band. There would be neither a profit or a loss at this point. Your hope is that as the entertainment catches on, sales will increase substantially above the break-even point.

Inspecting and Maintaining Equipment

Another key to making profits is reducing equipment repair costs. An effective maintenance program will more than pay for itself. It can help avoid accidents, reduce downtime, and add dollars to your profit line. Equipment failures often mean disappointed or inconvenienced customers, frustrated or injured employees, and harried managers. It makes sense to keep your equipment in top shape. Aside from the fact that repair calls are expensive, it is hard to find good service people.

Step 1. The first step in developing a maintenance program is to explain to all employees the need for the program, and the benefits it will bring. Unless everyone believes in the program and cooperates, it will not work well. Most people respond to safety benefits and labor-saving features, so stress those points.

Step 2. Develop a file folder for every piece of major equipment. Each folder should contain the name of the product, the manufacturer's name, the model year and style of each piece of equipment, the warranty form, the service agency's name, a record of service calls with costs and dates, the specification sheets, and owner's operating manual. While a number of smaller items can be combined in one folder, it is preferable to keep a separate folder for each major item.

Step 3. It is important to formalize the program by developing a checklist for inspections. With a list, no piece of equipment is overlooked, and each piece of equipment undergoes proper inspection.

Step 4. Develop a set of easy to understand and accessible maintenance procedures for each piece of equipment. It is a good idea to keep three copies of all procedures—one for employee use, a second one for the manager's file, and a third copy as a spare (you can be sure one will get lost).

Step 5. Assign the responsibility for the inspection of equipment to a specific person. The frequency and extent of inspections should be clearly understood. There should be no doubt about the process of reporting the results of inspections and following up on corrective actions.

Instituting an equipment maintenance program lets employees know that the company cares, and they will strive to ensure its success. Many attempts at reducing breakage and malfunctions of equipment fail because employees are not properly motivated to cooperate. This is clearly a case where management must set the tone by doing its part to ensure success of the program.

Action Guidelines

✔ Obtain a liquor list from a liquor store or dealer and select an initial inventory.

✔ Create an inventory sheet that includes all of the items in your initial inventory for taking physical inventories.

✔ Develop a perpetual inventory book (using a three-ring binder) with a separate stock record card dedicated to each brand of liquor carried in stock.

✔ Demonstrate your understanding of beverage turnover rates, by calculating the turnover rate for a bar with the figures shown below:

Beginning Inventory 11/1	$2,200
Purchases 11/1 –11/30	7,800
Ending Inventory 11/30	2,450

✔ Develop an equipment list and a maintenance sheet for each item on the list.

MANAGING YOUR EMPLOYEES

When a business bases its success on the performance of its employees—training them well, providing the right tools, and paying adequately—everyone wins. The business thrives, its employees earn more money and develop a sense of pride, and its customers are pleased.

In the food and beverage business, only the servers have actual contact with customers, but every employee in a bar or restaurant must focus on customer service. They must clearly understand how their jobs fit into the process of satisfying customers. This is a basic tenet of total quality management.

Customer Service Comes First

The manner in which a server approaches a customer, presents information, answers questions, and demonstrates an appreciation for the customer's patronage has a great influence on how much that customer will spend and how often they will return.

But equally important is the work that the customer does not see. A poorly prepared meal, a soiled glass, or a messy restroom may disgruntle a customer to the point that they will not return. What happens? They try another place, and if they have a pleasant experience, they continue to go there.

One bad experience can cause the loss of a significant amount of revenue. For example, if a lost customer patronized a bar three times a week, and spent an average of $10 each visit for food and drinks, that represents a revenue loss of $15,600 over a 10-year period. What makes the matter more acute is no one knows how many customers are lost, because they usually do not complain—they just disappear.

How to Get the Most from Your Employees

A good management will first identify its objectives, then determine ways to accomplish them; developing sound policies and conveying them clearly to all employees. Everyone will then know exactly what is expected and how to achieve the desired results.

Getting the most out of employees begins with hiring the best people you can afford, and

- training them properly,
- providing the equipment and work spaces they need to do their jobs well,
- letting them know that you care about how things are done and are aware of what happens,
- soliciting ideas for improvement and making them aware that they are important to the organization, and
- supervising them carefully.

Labor Turnover Rate

The rate at which employees terminate employment has an impact on the profitability of a business because the cost of replacing employees is very high. The true cost of high labor turnover is not often realized by employers. It includes the following:

- Cost of the exit interview time
- Possible unemployment compensation tax increase
- Cost of advertising the job openings
- Hidden cost of lost production due to the declining morale of the remaining employees who have to pick up the slack
- Cost of interviewing time
- Cost of training new employees

- Cost of inefficiencies and products wasted while the new employees learn their jobs

Labor turnover rates can be calculated by dividing the number of employees terminated during a given period of time by the number of jobs in the organization. Multiply by 100 to convert this ratio to a percentage.

$$\frac{\text{No. of employees that terminated } \times 100}{\text{No. of Jobs}} = \text{Labor Turnover Rate}$$

For example, if the Ticker Tape Bar & Grill had 5 of its 21 employees terminate employment last year, its labor turnover rate would be 23.8%.

$$\frac{5 \times 100}{21} = 23.8\%$$

Payroll Analysis

Another labor related concern is staff productivity. The hospitality business is very vulnerable to seasonal ups and downs, and employers must react quickly to changes in sales to protect their profitability.

Employee productivity can be measured as it relates to 1) the number of customers served per employee (covers per employee), 2) sales per employee, and 3) sales per hour worked.

These measures of productivity may be calculated as follows and are illustrated in Figure 7.1 on p. 96.

Covers per Employee = Covers Served ÷ No. of Employees
Sales per Employee = Sales ÷ No. of Employees
Sales per Hour Worked = Sales ÷ Actual Hours Worked

Initial Interviews

Care should be taken to hire the best people you can afford. Employment applications can be an important tool in this process, but care must be taken to avoid legal pitfalls concerning the type of information that may be asked. Generic employment application forms may be purchased, or you may design your own. If you choose to do the latter, consult your

Weekly Payroll Analysis								
Date week of	Sales	Covers Served	No. of Emp.	Actual Hours Worked	Payroll	Covers per Emp.	Sales per Emp.	Sales per Hour Worked
Nov. 9	$18,400	2,254	18	720	$2,450	125.2	$1,022.22	$25.55
Nov. 16	$16,540	2,038	19	760	$2,468	107.2	$870.52	$21.76
Nov. 23	$14,480	1,982	20	800	$2,595	99.1	$724.00	$18.10
Nov. 30	$14,910	1,973	20	800	$2,550	98.7	$745.50	$18.64
Dec. 7	$22,750	2,445	21	840	$2,675	116.4	$1,083.33	$27.08

Figure 7.1: Illustration of process for analyzing weekly payroll.

nearest Department of Labor office to make certain you are not violating any employment rules.

Interview job applicants thoroughly to avoid hiring people with undesirable traits. Following are some examples of behavior exhibited by some applicants that warrant scrutiny.

- Display any impatience at answering questions
- Avoid giving specific answers
- Have an untidy appearance
- Are noticeably impolite
- Become overly friendly or take liberties, such as lighting a cigarette without permission, or grabbing objects on your desk
- Give the appearance of an active alcohol or drug problem
- Have a record of past employment problems or have unexplained gaps in the chronology of their work experience

Exit Interviews

The purpose of having exit interviews is to determine if there are reasons for an employee's departure that might have been avoided or that signal necessary changes. Sometimes an employee will leave a job because it is boring. Knowing this, management may be able to reconfigure the job to make it more interesting. On occasion employees will leave a job because they see another employee doing something of which they disapprove and do not want to become involved. Exit interviews can sometimes reveal information that an employer could not otherwise obtain.

New Employee Orientations

Inform new employees immediately what you will expect of them and what they may expect of you. Orientation sessions are essential if you wish to convey information in a clear and consistent way to all employees. The content of the sessions are dependent upon the type and size of an organization, but certain kinds of information are of interest to all employees. Figure 7.2 (p. 98) is a checklist of orientation topics that might be covered, as applicable:

It is also important to list any and all actions that will result in termination of employment. You may want to give the following list to your employee or post it in an employee area.

- Drinking or using drugs on the job
- Stealing
- Being uncooperative with superiors
- Improper treatment of a customer
- Inability to work with others
- Giving away drinks or other products

Some items will only need to be touched upon, while others may require an explanation. In any case, the new employee should be given an opportunity to ask questions. A thorough orientation at the time of employment may avert employee problems at a later date.

Training Your Staff

A common mistake when new employees start on a job is to simply turn them over to a present employee for training. The problem with that practice is the bad habits of the present employee are passed on to the new person. In addition, typically less than 80 percent of an employee's knowledge tends to get passed on.

Figure 7.2:

Orientation Checklist

- ❏ History of the establishment
- ❏ Who the owner is
- ❏ Who the management personnel are and who the employee reports to and takes orders from
- ❏ Hours—regular work week, when and where posted
- ❏ Vacation policy—how much time and when
- ❏ Fringe benefits—insurance, sick days, etc.
- ❏ Meals, if applicable—when and what items
- ❏ Compensation—rate per hour and what deductions
- ❏ When is pay day
- ❏ Tardiness policy
- ❏ Absenteeism policy
- ❏ Smoking policy
- ❏ Coffee break policy
- ❏ How training will occur—when, where, and by whom
- ❏ Advancement policy
- ❏ Overtime policy—if allowed, who authorizes it
- ❏ Tip reporting policy
- ❏ Lost guest check policy
- ❏ Breakage policy
- ❏ Partial pay or loan policy
- ❏ Dress code
- ❏ Who will supply uniforms and how many?

- ❏ Who will launder uniforms?
- ❏ Deposits for uniforms, if required
- ❏ Appearance of employee—fingernails and cleanliness
- ❏ Policy on jewelry and hairnets
- ❏ Policy on types of shoes (for safety considerations)
- ❏ Employee evaluation policy—how, when, and by whom
- ❏ Probationary period and warning policy
- ❏ Detailed tour of establishment—including where to park, which restrooms to use, and where to enter and leave
- ❏ How to call in, in case of emergency—when and who to call (with phone numbers)
- ❏ Personal behavior
- ❏ Personal phone call policy
- ❏ Policy on patronizing the establishment before or after work hours
- ❏ What to do in case of accidents or fire
- ❏ Use of safety guards on equipment
- ❏ Portion control policy
- ❏ Holiday work policy
- ❏ How to handle customer complaints

If present employees train new workers, they should be given at least a minimum of instruction on how to do so. A four-step method of training has been used very effectively in industry and is applicable to any training situation. The four steps are show, tell, let do, and check back:

1. Show the employee how to do the task. Demonstrate it.
2. Simultaneously tell the employee what you are doing and why you are doing it.
3. Let the employee do it once, under supervision. If the employee does it right, allow them to continue on their own.
4. Check back to make sure the employee continues to do the task properly.

This technique is effective with such tasks as cash register training, where there are a number of small, but easy to forget steps involved.

Today, many bars will only hire people that have been trained at a professional bartending school because they want consistency of drinks and service. But, even with such training, new bartenders must be familiarized with management's policies before they start to work independently.

Providing the proper equipment to do a job is management's responsibility. It is inexcusable for bartenders to be overpouring or putting out inferior drinks simply because they lack the proper measuring tools. The physical arrangement of a bar is also important. A poorly laid-out bar can prevent a bartender from working efficiently.

How to Gain Your Employees' Cooperation

It is possible for an owner or manager to lead a somewhat normal life in the bar or restaurant business if they have loyal and cooperative employees. Regrettably, many operators are not so blessed, largely because they do not realize cooperation must be won, not dictated.

Following are six ways to win cooperation:

1. Make your employees want to cooperate with you. Let them know what your policies and objectives are. Let them know how they can personally benefit by working toward the accomplishment of your objectives. Appeal to their professional pride and desire to be on a winning team.

2. Do not expect unreasonable results. Set a fair challenge, but above all, be realistic.

3. Be open-minded to employees' suggestions and views. This shows you are concerned and sympathetic even when you have to say no.

4. Do not hesitate to give well-earned praise. If it is honest praise, the employee knows he deserves it. Acknowledging a good job, particularly on an undesirable task, is a good way of winning the employee's cooperation the next time you need to get a tough job done.

5. Avoid arguments with employees. Time has a calming effect—use it. Let the employee tell his or her side of the story and acknowledge that you heard it. Then arrange a time for discussion. Just a few minutes is often enough time for tempers to settle. Even the thorniest problems can be dealt with more easily when the parties involved are in control of their emotions.

6. Do not hesitate to admit an error on your part. It will not change your status or authority. Instead, it will humanize you in the eyes of your staff.

How to Improve Employee Morale

Low morale will inevitably result in poor work habits, waste, accidents, and, consequently, a loss of profits. Every aspect of a job contributes positively or negatively to the morale of the worker doing it. An effective manager will keep close watch on the morale of his or her organization and take corrective action quickly if it declines. Some ways to improve morale are listed below:

• Do not ignore false rumors.

• Discuss the impact of any proposed changes that will affect employees.

• Let your employees know how they are doing. Employees often believe they are overlooked when they do something well, but are immediately notified when they make a mistake. Try to eradicate that notion by giving them positive feedback as well as suggestions on how to correct any deficiencies.

- Be firm, but fair—make reasonable assignments and enforce rules in an impartial manner.

- Work through your chain-of-command—don't undercut your supervisors by throwing your weight around or by dealing directly with subordinate employees.

- Try to find out what every employee's strength or special skill is, and when possible give him or her the opportunity to use it.

- Provide employees with the environment to do a good job. This not only includes the proper tools but also sanitary and safe equipment, good lighting, sound control, and physical comforts (such as rubber floor mats on a hard tile floor).

- Be responsive to employees' concerns. You may not agree with them but do not try to avoid them. If the complaints are valid, they won't go away. In any case, explain the reasons for your thinking.

Keep the Lines of Communication Open

It is a good practice to discuss problems with your bar personnel on a regular basis. Issues such as high cost percentages, adverse customer comments, a critical health inspector's report can be better solved in an atmosphere of cooperation, where employees are allowed input.

Create an environment that will allow your employees to communicate with you. Hold weekly meetings—give them a chance to offer constructive ideas—but keep the meetings brief and businesslike. Have a written agenda ready—look organized, but not intimidating. Think of the meetings as a two-way street with information flowing from you to them and from them to you. It will be up to you to direct the discussion in order to keep it in a productive channel.

Conducting Staff Meetings

Meetings are effective only when they are preplanned and carefully executed. The leader must appear organized and convey the purpose of the meeting quickly, otherwise it will quickly degenerate to idle conversation. Figure 7.3 on p. 102 is a checklist for conducting meetings. You should review it periodically.

Figure 7.3:

Checklist for Efficient Meetings

❑ Do I have my material well organized?

❑ Do I seem to speak to one person, or do I make eye contact with everyone?

❑ Do I try to solicit views from employees who are less apt to speak out?

❑ Do I appear alert and enthusiastic?

❑ Do I set a good example with my speech and professional behavior?

❑ Am I supportive to employees who offer constructive suggestions?

❑ Do I avoid placing blame and embarrassing an employee in front of others?

Beware of Hidden Agendas

Try to eliminate any fears, jealousies, antagonisms, or misunderstandings among employees. These conflicts detract from an employee's performance and may be visible and objectionable to customers. When such a situation occurs, bring both parties together, confront the issue, and let them know how it is affecting their work. Seek agreement from both parties on the resolution of the problem.

Management's challenge is to instill a spirit of cooperation among all employees. Following are a few useful strategies for dealing with employees:

- Be friendly, but firm.
- Listen patiently to both sides of a story before judging.
- Be as tactful as possible.
- Explain thoroughly the reasons for your decision.
- Never argue in front of customers or other employees.
- Try to end discussions on a positive note.

Job Descriptions

Job descriptions are used for many purposes. Most notably, for identifying necessary tasks and proper procedures. Rarely, however, do non-

Bar Manager

Summary

Responsible to the owner. Oversees the day-to-day operations of the bar (both front-of-house and back-of-house). Responsible for implementing company policies and performing the following duties: purchasing liquors, wines, and beers; hiring and training new employees; supervising and motivating staff; performing control functions; and maintaining a high level of quality and service in all aspects of the operation.

Responsibilities

1. Performs all assigned duties and responsibilities according to company policies and reports to the owner in a timely and efficient manner.

2. Researches and purchases products necessary to satisfy customers' wants and needs, and the sales objectives of the establishment.

3. Responsible for cost control programs in the areas of payroll, food, beverages, supplies, and utilities so that maximum quality is obtained at minimum cost.

4. Coordinates bar service for functions.

5. Supervises and motivates employees.

6. Inspects bar and lounge operations regularly for cleanliness and proper functioning of equipment.

7. Inspects the bar and lounge during all rush periods to ensure that proper service is being given to customers.

8. Assists, as needed, in all capacities and handles customers' complaints.

9. Schedules bar and lounge employees to ensure high quality service while containing payroll cost within an established percentage range.

10. Responsible for hiring and terminating employees, processing time cards, evaluating employees, and conducting training sessions, as necessary.

11. Responsible for safety and security systems at the bar.

12. Responsible for sanitation in all areas.

13. Auditions and contracts appropriate entertainment (with the approval of the owner).

14. Responsible for taking inventories and calculating bar cost percentages.

15. Responsible for maximizing food and beverage sales through proper pricing and effective advertising and sales promotional efforts.

Figure 7.4: Sample Job Description.

management employees receive a job description when they are hired. This is unfortunate because the new employee is the person who could benefit most from knowing what is expected. A job description can also serve as an excellent checklist when training a new employee.

A sample job description for a bar manager is shown in Figure 7.4 on p. 103 for illustrative purposes. As with all jobs, the duties of a bar manager will vary depending on the size of the operation, the type of bar, and the degree of autonomy the owner grants the manager. Frequently, in the case of small bars, the owner is also the manager. The list of the duties and responsibilities specified in Figure 7.4 are typical for most bars.

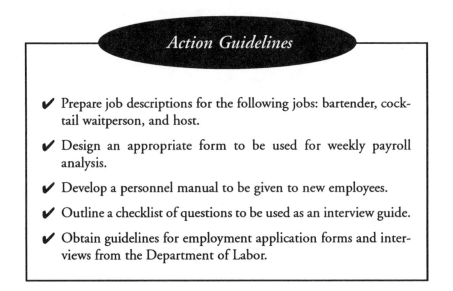

Action Guidelines

✔ Prepare job descriptions for the following jobs: bartender, cocktail waitperson, and host.

✔ Design an appropriate form to be used for weekly payroll analysis.

✔ Develop a personnel manual to be given to new employees.

✔ Outline a checklist of questions to be used as an interview guide.

✔ Obtain guidelines for employment application forms and interviews from the Department of Labor.

FINANCIAL CONTROL
OF THE BUSINESS

Two financial statements are the most commonly used tools for controlling a business, the income statement (also known as the profit and loss statement) and the balance sheet. The income statement reports what you earned or lost. The balance sheet reports what you own, owe, and are worth.

A balance sheet is like a candid snapshot of your business, capturing an instant in time. The income statement is like a movie. It has a beginning, an ending (which is your profit or loss), and a middle, which explains what happened along the way. It is critical for a businessperson to understand these two statements. When you are considering corrective actions or future plans, your income statement and balance sheet will guide your decisions.

Understanding the Income Statement

In their simplest form, all income statements cover four basic areas of information—revenues, costs, expenses, and profits. Put another way, they tell you how much money you took in, how much you paid out, and the difference between the two, which will be a net gain or loss. For example,

Total Revenues	$762,998
Less: Costs	191,700
Expenses	453,388
Net Profit Before Federal Income Tax	$117,910

The scant version has some value, but is very limited in its ability to point out problems and suggest improvements. Only when an income statement is fleshed out, as shown in Figure 8.1, with details and percentages, can management use it as an analytical tool.

What Your Income Statement Tells You

Beyond the numbers, an income statement can show relationships between categories, such as net profit to sales, and costs and expenses to sales. These relationships are expressed as percentages. When compared with an income statement for a previous period, it can reflect progress or decline. It can also raise a number of questions about a business.

- Is the business undergoing unintended changes? Is it selling more liquor than food, or more food than liquor?
- Have product costs in relation to sales gotten out of line?
- Are the various categories of expenses excessive when compared to industry standards for comparable businesses?
- Is the business generating an acceptable level of income?
- Are any trends emerging?

These questions lead to other questions that systematically isolate problems and suggest solutions. For example, if product costs (as a percentage of sales) have gotten out of line, management must find out why. That raises a set of questions. Is it due to carelessness and waste, lack of training, poor purchasing practices, inadequate pricing of drinks, or pilferage? Management must then look at each of those specific areas in detail, and locate the reason for the high product costs. At that point, the corrective action associated with the problem will become apparent.

Understanding the Balance Sheet

A *balance sheet* is a statement of what you own and owe to others, as well as, a declaration of what your business interest is worth. Figure 8.2 on p. 108 is an example.

Analyzing Statements

There are numerous accounting tools for analysis. Many of them are better left to accountants, but 11of them in particular are useful to bar own-

Income Statement
for the period of January 1 through December 31, 199—

			Pct.
Sales			
Food Sales	$395,572		52.0%
Beverage Sales	$365,144		48.0
Total Sales		$760,716	100.0
Cost of Sales			
Food Cost	$138,450		35.0
Beverage Cost	83,983		23.0
Total Cost of Sales		$222,433	29.2
Gross Profit from Operations		$538,283	70.8
Other Income		2,282	0.3
Total Income		$540,565	71.1
Controllable Expenses			
Payroll	$200,829		26.4
Employee Benefits	30,429		4.0
Direct Operating Expenses	43,361		5.7
Advertising and Promotion	22,061		2.9
Music and Entertainment	15,214		2.0
Utilities	24,343		3.2
Administrative and General Expenses	30,429		4.0
Repairs and Maintenance	15,214		2.0
Total Controllable Expenses		$381,880	50.2
Profit Before Occupancy Costs		$158,685	20.9
Occupancy Costs (Triple Net Lease)			
Rent	$38,796		5.1
Property Taxes	4,564		0.6
Other Taxes	1,521		0.2
Property Insurance	7,607		1.0
Total Occupancy Costs		$52,488	6.9
Profit Before Interest and Depreciation		$106,197	14.0
Interest		3,804	0.5
Depreciation		15,216	2.0
Net Profit Before Taxes		87,177	11.5
Federal Income Taxes		$ 29,056	3.8
NET PROFIT After Federal Income Taxes		$ 58,121	7.7

Figure 8.1: Sample Income Statement.

Balance Sheet

December 31, 199__

Assets

Current Assets

Cash on Hand	$4,000	
Cash in Bank	48,000	
Accounts Receivable	3,500	
Food	8,850	
Inventory		
Beverage Inventory	8,650	
Supplies Inventory	2,500	
Marketable Securities	44,106	
Prepaid Expenses	12,500	
Total Current Assets		**$132,106**

Fixed Assets

Furniture, Fixtures & Equipment	$129,694		
Less: Depreciation Reserve	25,000	104,694	
Leasehold Improvements	64,480		
Less: Depreciation Reserve	1,280	63,200	
Total Fixed Assets			**167,894**
Total Assets			**300,000**

Liabilities and Net Worth

Current Liabilities

Accounts Payable	13,000	
Taxes Collected	6,500	
Accrued Expenses	14,455	
Federal Income Tax	11,045	
Current Portion of Long-Term Loan Due	1,886	
Total Current Liabilities		**46,886**

Long-Term Loan Balance (12%)	105,000	
Less: Current Portion Due	1,886	
Total Long-Term Loan		**103,114**

Net Worth

Partner A—Capital	75,000	
Partner B—Capital	75,000	
Total Partner's Net Worth		**150,000**
Total Liabilities and Net Worth		**$300,000**

Figure 8.2: Sample Balance Sheet.

ers and managers. They measure the health of a business, signal problems that need attention, and point out strengths and weaknesses.

1. Pouring Cost Percentage (PC)
2. Food Cost Percentage
3. Labor Cost Percentage
4. Expense Percentages
5. Net Profit on Sales
6. Rate of Return on Investment
7. Current Ratio
8. Acid Test Ratio
9. Working Capital
10. Average Guest Check
11. Seat Turnover Rate

Statistical data on operating costs may be obtained from the National Restaurant Association in Chicago, IL and the National Licensed Beverage Association in Alexandria, VA.

Pouring Cost Percentage (PC). This tells you what percentage of the selling price of a drink goes to pay for the ingredients required to make it. The percentage can be calculated for one drink, or for all of the liquor sold in a given period of time. Depending on style of service, sales promotional objectives, and efficiency, percentages typically range from 18% to 30%. The formula for calculating a pouring cost percentage follows:

Cost of Beverages Sold ÷ Beverage Sales = Pouring Cost Percentage
Example: $83,983 ÷ $365,144 = 23%

Food Cost Percentage. This tells you what percentage of the selling price of a food item or a meal goes to pay for the ingredients required to make it. Like the pouring cost percentage, it can be calculated for a single item or for all the food sold in a given period of time. Percentages for most table service operations range from 30% to 40%, depending on style of service, sales promotional objectives, and efficiency. Food cost percentages are calculated as follows:

Cost of Food Sold ÷ Food Sales = Food Cost Percentage
Example: $138,450 ÷ $395,572 = 35%

Labor Cost Percentage. This tells you what percentage of sales goes to pay your labor costs. It gives you an indication of how efficiently you are using your work force. If the percentage is high when compared to industry standards for similar establishments, you may be overstaffing, paying too much overtime, or not planning and supervising jobs well enough. The formula for calculating your labor cost percentage follows:

(Payroll + Employee Benefits) ÷ Total Sales = Labor Cost Percentage
Example: ($200,829 + $30,429) ÷ $760,716 = 30.4%

Expense Percentages. This indicates how well operating expenses are being controlled. There are many categories of expense that can be abused if not supervised carefully. Linens can be used improperly, lights can be left on in empty rooms, heat may not be turned down at night, paper goods may be wasted, or advertising expenditures may not be producing results. Most expenses are controllable. The following formula may be used to determine the relationship of any expense item to total sales:

Expense ÷ Total Sales = Expense Percentage
(Utilities) $24,343 ÷ $760,716 = 3.2%

Percentage of Net Profit on Sales. This is important, because it summarizes the overall ability of a business to operate profitably. Some businesses take in a great deal of revenue but do a poor job of controlling costs and expenses, and consequently make very little profit. This percentage relates profits to sales. It can also be calculated on an after-tax basis, by using the net profit amount after taxes.

Net Profit Before Tax ÷ Total Sales = Percentage of Net Profit on Sales
$87,177 ÷ $760,716 = 11.5%

Rate of Return on Investment. This is a measure of how well a business is profiting when compared to the funds invested, or how well it is paying back the investors. It is a very important piece of information to consider when buying or selling a business. It is also useful when comparing alternative investment opportunities.

Net Profit After Tax ÷ Investment = Rate of Return on Investment
$58,121 ÷ $300,000 = 19.4%

Current Ratio. This is of interest to suppliers and lenders. It reflects a firm's ability to pay its bills as they come due. Only assets consumed and replenished in the ongoing conduct of a business may be used in this calculation. Those assets, called current assets, include cash, receivables, marketable securities, inventories, and prepaid expenses (such as insurance premiums paid in advance). The current ratio relates current assets to current liabilities. Current liabilities include only those obligations that are payable on a current basis, such as accounts payable, notes payable, and accrued expenses (example, wages payable). The formula for calculating a current ratio is as follows:

$$\text{Current Assets} \div \text{Current Liabilities} = \text{Current Ratio}$$
$$\$132,106 \div \$46,886 = 2.8{:}1$$

In the above example, the firm has 2.8 times as many current assets, as it has current liabilities. A ratio of at least 2 to 1 is generally believed to provide adequate assurance that current bills can be paid in a timely manner.

The Acid Test Ratio. This is calculated in instances where a business does not have the desired minimum current ratio of 2 to 1. Only certain "quick" assets may be counted in the calculation of the acid test ratio—cash and assets that can be quickly converted into cash, namely accounts receivable and marketable securities. The sum of those three quick assets is divided by current liabilities, as shown below:

$$\frac{\text{Cash} + \text{Accounts Receivable} + \text{Marketable Securities}}{\text{Current Liabilities}} = \text{Acid Test Ratio}$$

$$\frac{\$52,000 + \$3,500 + \$44,106}{\$44,886} = 2.2{:}1$$

In the above example the firm has 2.2 times as many quick assets as it has current liabilities. This shows it to be in excellent financial condition and very capable of paying its current obligations when due. A 1 to 1 ratio is the minimum desired for the acid test.

Working Capital. This is a measurement of the funds available to run the ongoing affairs of a business. Lack of working capital is one of the more common reasons for business failures. Some entrepreneurs spend so much of their money on buildings and equipment that they have difficulty paying bills while their business is developing a cash flow. Working capital is the difference between a firm's total of current assets and its total current liabilities.

Current Assets - Current Liabilities = Working Capital
$132,106 - $46,886 = $85,220

Average Guest Check. This calculation tells how much each customer tends to spend when he or she patronizes your establishment. A declining guest check average may indicate that the quality of your food or drinks is slipping, or that your wait staff is not practicing suggestive selling. Appetizers, desserts, and after dinner drinks can double a guest check, but they need to be mentioned enthusiastically by wait staff. The average guest check is calculated as follows:

Total Sales ÷ No. of Guests Served = Average Guest Check
$760,716 ÷ 42,262 = $18

Seat Turnover Ratio. This is an indicator of how successfully you are drawing people to your establishment. A low, or declining seat turnover ratio is of concern, because it represents an erosion of the customer base. If not corrected, the business may fail. The following formula shows how a seat turnover ratio can be calculated. In this example, the 100 seats were filled 1.7 times a day on average.

No. of Customers Annually ÷ No. of Seats ÷ 365 days = Seat Turnover
Ratio

62,140 ÷ 100 ÷ 365 = 1.7 times a day

Trends

Food and beverage cost percentages may be calculated daily, weekly, or monthly. The maximum recommended period is one month. Beyond that, results become increasingly less useful for solving problems. Some cost control systems calculate daily, weekly, and monthly percentages. Weekly and monthly percentages are more indicative of emerging trends than are a single day's percentage, because good days average out bad days. Consequently, when you have a high monthly percentage, you know you have a more serious problem. On a daily basis, numbers may be inconclusive. For instance, if there was an unexpected storm one day and no one came to eat at your bar, that day's food cost percentage would be unusually high because a lot of food was prepared but very little sold. The next day when you run out the carry-over food, there would be an offsetting low food cost percentage, because you would have normal sales with virtually no new food used.

The same applies to liquor. For example, an accidentally broken bottle of whiskey can cause a glaring rise in one day's pouring cost percentage, but when viewed in the context of a whole week's business, it does not give cause for alarm. It is advisable as a matter of policy, however, to check out the reason for any drastic increase in the percentage.

Trends are of greater concern to management because they represent entrenched practices and greater losses. If not corrected, they will get worse and therefore cannot be allowed to continue.

How Much Control is Enough?

A saying in the business is "the cost of controls should not exceed the savings they can make." In other words, do not spend dollars to chase after pennies. Every business has its own special circumstances that will dictate how much control is enough.

If an owner is actively involved in a business, a greater amount of personal control will be present. Hence, a lesser amount of formal control will be needed. As opposed to that, operations with absentee owners must have very tight controls because their profit potential and investment are at stake.

Two problems can arise, in the case of the active owner, if no controls are utilized. One is the owner may become enslaved to the business, for fear of leaving it in someone else's hands. And two, unless the owner is present every minute of every day, the business is vulnerable during any unattended periods. Controls require a little effort but can render a great deal of peace of mind and freedom. Large chain organizations have proved that with adequate controls, training and supervision, businesses can be run very well with absentee ownership.

A Simple Cost System for a Small Bar

Some small bars have no controls, because they do not want more paperwork. For those bars, the simple control system illustrated below would be a substantial improvement. It requires only three procedures:

1. A periodic inventory
2. A record of purchases
3. A record of sales

An inventory is taken at the beginning of a period, and again at the end of the period. The duration of the period may be from one week to a month but should not exceed a month. During the period, a record of sales and purchases is kept. At the end of the period the following calculations are made:

Beginning Inventory	6/1	$2,800
Plus: Purchases	6/1–6/30	5,400
Total		8,200
Less: Ending Inventory	6/30	3,200
Cost of Beverages Sold		$5,000

$$\frac{\text{Cost of Beverages Sold}}{\text{Beverage Sales}} = \frac{\$5,000}{\$25,000} = 20\% \text{ Pouring Cost}$$

Unless the owner wants to work from opening to closing every day, a minimal amount of control such as that illustrated above should be installed. The pouring cost percentage is a measure of the bar's efficiency. Careless pouring, giving drinks away, waste, and pilferage are all reasons why a pouring cost percentage might go up.

Identifying Undesirable Practices

No matter how well management tries to screen applicants and hire good people, the possibility exists that undesirable practices may set in and result in a loss of profits and customers. Management must monitor operations carefully to deter or at least quickly discover such activities. Here are examples of unethical or illegal behaviors that directly affect your bottom line.

- Adding water to bottles to conceal shortages
- Substituting cheaper liquors for more expensive ones

- Serving drinks to other employees without charging them
- Overpouring to get bigger tips
- Giving free drinks or unauthorized discounts to friends
- Changing inventory counts to cover up for merchandise taken undetected
- Receiving kickbacks from suppliers in return for buying their merchandise and not turning them in to the management
- Accepting gifts in return for buying inferior or overpriced products
- Drinking while on duty
- Tampering with counters or meters on machines or bottles
- Faking lost guest checks, petty cash pay-outs, or breakage
- Leaving the cash register drawer open and not ringing up every sale

Automated Beverage Dispensing Systems

There is a wide variety of dispensing systems on the market today. Some are completely automatic, and others are little more than bottle pourers with built-in counting devices.

The degree to which a bar will automate, will depend upon the size and volume of the establishment, its available funds, and its management's perception of its control problems and the bar's potential. Many reasons for installing automatic dispensing systems are put forth by their manufacturers, the most prominent being such benefits as:

- Mixing perfectly blended cocktails
- Dispensing drinks uniformly and consistently
- Preventing overpouring and spillage
- Eliminating pricing errors
- Insuring drinks will not be given away
- Removing temptation
- Controlling inventories

Though not infallible, there is no question about the capability of completely automated systems to control inventories. They can also reveal missing guest checks and cash shortages. Users regard them highly. But, as good as automatic dispensing systems are, they are not without their critics. The main criticisms are:

- They are costly and in some cases expensive to install.
- They are perceived as impersonal and miserly by many customers.

How Do the Systems Work?

Each system has its proprietary differences, but in general, beverages are poured from spouts, guns, or devices attached to individual bottles. As the system pours, the quantity of beverage dispensed is counted by a meter or a computer.

The number and types of functions a system will perform vary with cost. Some systems measure and count, while others store vast amounts of data and perform analytical calculations as well. Cash registers may be integrated into the systems to provide inventory and sales reports. Examine potential savings and benefits carefully before investing in any system.

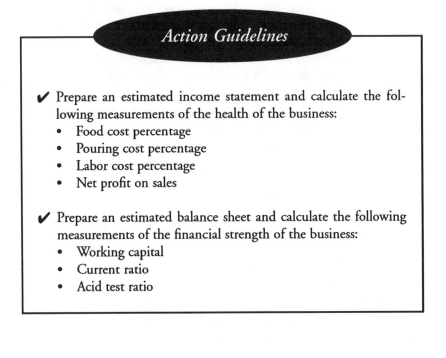

Action Guidelines

✔ Prepare an estimated income statement and calculate the following measurements of the health of the business:
- Food cost percentage
- Pouring cost percentage
- Labor cost percentage
- Net profit on sales

✔ Prepare an estimated balance sheet and calculate the following measurements of the financial strength of the business:
- Working capital
- Current ratio
- Acid test ratio

MARKETING

A simple definition of marketing is to get the right goods or services to the right customers, at the right time and place, and at the right price. The key word in each instance is right, and a marketing plan will help you make the right decisions.

Why Do You Need a Marketing Plan?

A marketing plan keeps your marketing activities on track. It identifies your goals and focuses the actions of all employees in a concerted effort to achieve your desired objectives. It removes guesswork and creates a stable atmosphere. When clearly communicated to all employees, it creates a team spirit that brings out the best qualities of everyone. Figure 9.1 on p. 118 breaks the development of a marketing plan into seven steps.

Marketing activities include a broad range of tools, called the marketing mix. They include market research, product and concept development, packaging, pricing, advertising and sales promotion, and personal selling strategies. Successful marketing programs start with an in-depth knowledge of prospective customers' wants and needs.

Know Your Business Life Cycle

Most businesses pass through a life cycle, as summarized in Figure 9.2 (p. 119). It is essential at each stage to know where you are at, because your marketing activities should be based on what is required at each stage.

Figure 9.1:

A Seven Step Process
for Developing a Marketing Plan

1. Establish your overall objective.
   Example: To increase sales by 50% next year.

2. Identify your strengths and weaknesses.
   Strengths   Weaknesses
   Excellent food and drinks   Lack of seating capacity
   Excellent service

3. List the alternative strategies available to you.
   (i)   Add on to existing building.
   (ii) Attract more people on slow nights.
   (iii) Get people to come earlier and/or stay later.

4. Select the best strategy.
   Assume that attracting more people on slow nights (ii) is the best strategy.

5. Develop a detailed plan of action.
   (i)   Conduct a survey to learn what attracts people most.
   (ii) Have a different theme planned for each normally slow night.
   (iii) Establish a timetable.
   (iv) Hire entertainment.
   (v)   Advertise the events.

6. Implement the plans.
   (i)   Start doing it.
   (ii) Keep careful records of results.
   (iii) Observe the good and bad points of what you are doing.
   (iv) Refine and adjust specific actions, as you go along.
   (v)   Reinforce the good features.
   (vi) Correct the flaws.

7. Evaluate the results of your efforts.
   Decide whether to continue or terminate the program.

Figure 9.2:

The Business Life Cycle

Life Cycle Stage	Characteristics of that Stage
1. Introduction	Your business has just started. You are trying to survive and become established. Systems are being perfected.
2. Conservative Growth	A period of slow and steady growth of sales as more people learn about your establishment. You try new ideas to attract more people.
3. Rapid Growth	Your reputation spreads. The word is out that you have a unique concept and serve good food and drinks. Your popularity grows rapidly, as do your sales. Competitors notice your success.
4. Leveled Maturity	Competition intensifies as others copy your ideas, and new competitors emerge. Growth ceases and you try to hold your market share.
5. Rejuvenation or Decline	Competitors and new entrants not only take your ideas but improve on them. You must reinvent your business, again introducing new ideas that differentiate and position you ahead of the pack, or your business will decline.

In Stage 1, a business would focus its advertising on letting the public know it exists, what it offers, and where it is. In Stages 2 and 3, its advertising would change to promotions that would bring in first-time patrons and increase patronage by existing customers. In Stage 4, it would attempt to hold its market share by capitalizing on the reputation it built in the previous three stages. It would remind people about its quality and the reasons it became popular. In Stage 5, if successful in rejuvenating itself, its advertising would emphasize what is new or improved. Essentially, the whole process would start over for the new product.

Market Research

There are three types of information about prospective customers that can help a business plan a marketing strategy.

1. Demographic information
2. Geographic information
3. Psychographic information

Demographics are facts about people, such as their age, income, education, occupation, race, religion, nationality. The more you know about the population in your marketing area, the better you will be able to serve them. You will be aware of their customs and special holidays—when, where, and how they spend their money, how you should price your menu, and what level of service will be expected of you.

Geographic information tells you where people live and work. It will tell you something about their dining and drinking patterns. For example, harried commuters are more apt to rush to their cars after work, than in-town dwellers.

Psychographic information deals with lifestyles and motivational influences on people's spending behavior. It can tell you such things as whether people are name brand conscious, are influenced by peer groups, are socially oriented and have a need to keep up with others.

It is possible to buy market information, if you can afford it. There are firms that constantly conduct market research and sell their findings to businesses. Their names are available at the reference department of your local library and in business and telephone directories.

If you cannot afford to buy data, you can gather a great deal of information on your own, through observation and discreet questioning. Public information agencies such as chambers of commerce, state and city offices, as well as newspapers and radio stations can provide much information.

In addition to researching your prospective customers, check out your competition. The success of a competitor may be an indicator of how well you will do. It is also a good way to cross-fertilize your own ideas.

Study the economic trend of your community. Focus on where it is headed, not on what it was like in the past—for as investment advisors are prone to say, past history is no guarantee of future performance. Your market research will influence decisions that may make or break you.

Following is a list of questions that should be answered by your research:

- What kinds of competition are there in your proposed marketing area? What are your competitors offering? Menu? Style of service? Entertainment? Atmosphere and decor?
- How successful are your competitors?
- What kinds of customers do they attract?
- What special things are they doing to attract their clientele?
- What are their merchandising and pricing policies?
- What are their apparent strengths and weaknesses?

You cannot be sure your concept is truly unique until you research your competitors. Recognizing your competitors' strengths will stimulate your creative processes and inspire you to do your best. After examining competitors' merchandising styles and target markets, you can devise your own marketing strategies to reach your desired clientele. By assessing the intensity of the competition, you will have some idea of the degree of difficulty you can expect in your effort to penetrate the market.

The most direct way to gather information about your competitors is to patronize their establishments. Observe carefully. Chat with waitstaff. Question suppliers and delivery people. Talk to other business owners, and anyone else who might give you valuable information. Don't be bashful about your research efforts, you can be sure your competitors will be researching your business as soon as you open. Everything you learn will help you develop a competitive strategy and capitalize on their weaknesses. Below are some things to look at when researching another bar or restaurant.

- Type of bar or restaurant
- Capacity of the establishment
- Waiting time to be seated and then to be served
- Efficiency and friendliness of the host/maître d'
- Wine, liquor, and food menus
- Quality of food and drinks
- Cost in relation to quality
- Variety of offerings
- Setup of tables

- Decor of rooms
- Overall cleanliness of the facility
- Availability of wait staff when needed
- Nonsmoking sections provided
- Noise level
- General ambiance of establishment
- Sales promotional techniques utilized—displays, price inducements, personal selling
- Accuracy of bill and timeliness of presentation
- Promptness in collecting your payment

Identifying Your Target Market

Most businesses in the public hospitality field want everyone to feel welcome in their establishment. As a result, they often make the mistake of thinking their target market is everyone. When in fact, their target market is that segment of the population that strongly wants what they offer or is most apt to patronize their establishment.

Everyone does not want the same thing. People over 45 do not generally have the same tastes for music or ambiance as people in their early 20s have. Most bars and restaurants have a stronger following within certain demographic groups. The best way to identify your target market is to segment the market according to demographic, geographic, and psychographic variables as shown in Figure 9.3.

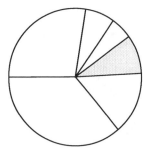

= Target Market

- Professionals
- Age 25-50
- Income over $30,000
- Live in city

Figure 9.3: Sample Customer Profile.

Clarifying Your Customers' Wants and Needs

Supplement your own observation by researching hospitality industry trade journals. Popularity indexes of food and drink preferences are periodically published by trade journals. The National Restaurant Association also compiles data on customer spending patterns and other industry statistics, providing valuable information on the performance of eating and drinking establishments in its annual publication *Restaurant Industry Operations Report.*

Identify your customers' wants or needs when they come to your establishment, and identify how you can satisfy their wants or needs. Many bars have two distinct types of clientele. In the daytime they cater to workers, shoppers, and tourists; and at night they cater to a social, fun-seeking clientele. Careful planning will allow you to serve both groups without sacrificing your desired image. Figure 9.4 illustrates how customer wants and needs may be analyzed.

Figure 9.4:

Customer Analysis

Type of Guest	Want or Need	Response
Workers, lunchtime	Nourishment	Good, healthy food
Workers, after work	Relaxation	Comfortable seating, soft music
Dinner guests, tourists, visitors	Excitement	Interesting food, exotic drinks
Entertainment seekers	Stimulation	Music, dancing
Social guests	Meet people	Informal setting, stand-up bars

Competitive Strategies

There are three types of competitive strategies you may consider as a result of your research findings. The first is a *cost-based market penetration strategy*—that is, you can penetrate the market with lower prices than your competitors. This is a popular strategy, but it is feasible only when accompanied by tight cost controls and cost-minimization efforts in all expense areas so you can still make a profit and survive.

If you do not have any competition, you may charge what the traffic will bear (a practice referred to as *skimming the market*) for as long as your offering is in demand, and until competitors appear. It is essential, however, to be aware of your *pricing points.* Those are limits—prices above which customers do not perceive your product or service to be worth what you are charging.

The second strategy is a *differentiation strategy,* which refers to distinguishing in your customers' mind your business apart from your competitors. You can differentiate your business by advertising its uniqueness or high quality. Uniqueness can take many forms. A bar's unusual atmosphere and decor, music, specialized style of service, or menu offerings can differentiate it from its competitors. You can also make your business appear to be different simply by the way you position your competitors' products in your advertising. An example of this would be the following statement in an advertisement: "PLAY SMART—NOW YOU CAN DINE AND DANCE IN A SMOKE-FREE BAR, WITH A HEALTHY MENU!" If competitors allowed smoking and offered only deep-fried, fast foods, this bar would appear different to its target market.

The third strategy is *concentration,* which is focusing on a particular customer group, geographic location, or style of service. While the cost-based and differentiation strategies are aimed at the entire potential market, the concentration strategy aims at a particular need of a specific segment of your target market.

How to Get New Customers

Some customers will patronize your establishment because you are conveniently located. Others will come to your bar because it is the new place in town or because they have heard good things about it. But many will intend to come to your place someday and yet will never get around to doing so, unless you do something special to draw them in.

Consumers, knowingly or unknowingly, go through a decision-making process before making purchases. They pass through five stages, and the same process often applies to people who try a new bar or restaurant. The process may be depicted as follows:

1. Awareness: when a person first realizes you exist
2. Interest: develops when they hear something good about your place from a friend
3. Evaluation: occurs as they mull over what they have heard and decide whether or not to try it sometime
4. Trial: when the customer visits your bar to see if he or she like it
5. Adoption or Rejection: the result of the customer's first experience at your establishment

The consumer's decision-making process indicates how hard it is to get regular customers, and the importance of taking good care of your present customers. They are both a source of income and valuable word of mouth advertising.

To get new customers, you must first make them aware of your existence through advertising and sales promotion programs and, better yet, pleasing your present customers so they will tell their friends about your establishment. Without question, the most effective advertising a business can have is word of mouth advertising from satisfied customers.

The Grand Opening

People are attracted to grand openings. They represent something new, perhaps a better deal. The grand opening is the most important time for a bar or restaurant to do things right. This is when you can really impress new customers and leave them bubbling with satisfaction and ready to tell their friends about the great new place they discovered. Unfortunately, many establishments waste the opportunity to cash in on their grand opening and in some cases it takes months to recover from an initial flurry of bad word of mouth advertising. Below are some ways to make a grand opening successful.

- Do not have a grand opening until you are ready to do everything right. Carefully plan a schedule of preliminary activities to ensure you will be ready on the designated date of the grand opening.
- Conduct thorough training of your front-of-the-house staff and your back-of-the-house staff prior to the grand opening.
- Test all equipment to make sure it is properly assembled, clean, and functional. Do so adequately in advance to allow tradespeople time to come back and make corrections if necessary.

- Make sure all of your licenses and permits are in place before the grand opening date. More than one opening has had to be postponed because of a last minute snag. Work closely with the licensing authorities.

- Coordinate deliveries in advance with all of your suppliers to avoid distractions, shortages, or returned merchandise on the day of the grand opening.

- Have a private party before going public with your grand opening. A function where you invite your relatives and close friends, business associates, and anyone who can ever do you any good—such as media people, suppliers, politicians, liquor, fire, and health authorities, lenders and investors, and contractors. The event is free so you can expect a high rate of attendance.

   This is a chance to strut your stuff in a friendly atmosphere. No one will complain if something goes wrong at this event, because the price is right, and they are all people who are interested in seeing you succeed. Nonetheless, every detail including mistakes and problems should be handled as though the people were paying guests. The purpose of this function is to iron out wrinkles, and since it is your final exam, it should be done smoothly.

The best planned grand opening will be of little value if people do not know about it. You must advertise and publicize it well in advance, so that people can talk it up with their friends and make plans to try your establishment. A frequently used technique for announcing your grand opening with a big splash is to have all of your contractors and suppliers sponsor a large newspaper advertisement that congratulates you on your opening and wishes you well. The contractors have made money on you and the suppliers will make a lot of money on you in the future, if you are successful, so it is in their interest to do this. Besides, it places their name in the public's eye as well and serves as an advertisement for their business. Everybody wins.

Other things that should be done to announce a grand opening are:

- Visit all nearby merchants to introduce yourself. Other businesses are frequently asked by their customers for restaurant and bar recommendations.

- Send a direct mailing to all businesses within your dominant marketing area. Include a copy of your menu and information about your hours and offerings. Be sure to emphasize your name and address prominently, so that if the recipient does not read the entire mailing, they will at least know who you are and where you are.

- Make contact with any visitor information centers in your community. Leave appropriate literature for their information racks.

- Put an eye catching "Coming Soon" sign in your front window announcing the date of the grand opening. This should be done well in advance, to attract the attention of the most people possible.

Free Publicity

The print media welcomes newsworthy publicity releases from businesses. On slow news days editors who have the responsibility of filling many pages with print will use press releases. Publicity articles can be about a wide variety of things, such as grand openings of new businesses, new products, a significant contribution to a charity, an award from a professional association, a change of name, or a promotion of a key person. They cannot be blatantly self-serving, or contain unsubstantiated claims, or be critical of other products. In short, they cannot be advertisements. But, if they are genuinely newsworthy, well-written, and submitted on time, they stand an excellent chance of being published.

Free publicity is more valuable than paid advertising, because readers tend to believe news articles much more than advertisements. Many people do not realize publicity articles are very often written by the business they describe.

Photographs make publicity articles much more interesting. They increase the readership rate dramatically and, if of good quality, editors like to run them. It is worth trading a meal and a couple of drinks to have a professional photographer take a picture for you. The quality of their prints is beyond what most people could produce, and they know how to compose a subject.

Following are some tips for writing successful publicity articles:

- Find out your local newspapers' deadlines for copy. Submit time-sensitive articles adequately in advance of the papers' deadline.

- Send articles to the appropriate editor. For example, an article on the sponsorship of a softball team should be sent to the sports editor, while an article announcing the appointment of a new manager should be sent to the business editor.

- Articles should be typed, double-spaced, on plain white paper. However, if you have a really important news story that cannot wait, telephone the editor.

- Use the five W's when writing publicity articles. In the first paragraph summarize the WHO, WHY, WHAT, WHEN, WHERE, and HOW of the story. Then proceed to give the details in subsequent paragraphs. If people read only the first paragraph, they will at least know your name and the important facts.

- In the case of a longer article, let the editor know if it was written exclusively for his or her paper.

- If the article is not time sensitive, indicate it is "submitted for publication on a space available basis." This gives it a greater chance of being published.

- Where possible, try to run a paid advertisement on the same page that the publicity article (and photograph) appears. You can make claims and self-serving statements in your ad. The credence given to the publicity article and its proximity to your paid ad will tend to transfer to what is said in the paid ad, giving its claims greater acceptance.

If public speaking is your cup of tea, take advantage of this excellent opportunity to relate to the community. Many groups are constantly looking for interesting speakers and would love to have a presentation on wines, beers, or the history of taverns. It is a good way to make acquaintances, elevate the image of your establishment, and get additional publicity—speaking events usually are announced by the sponsoring group in a press release.

The Ongoing Campaign—Keep Them Coming Back

Customers enjoy being catered to. Special attention makes them feel appreciated and interested in coming back soon. There are many ways to give special attention to customers. A friendly greeting when they arrive and a thank you and good-bye when they leave make their visit much more personal. This is especially effective when done by the owner or manager—everyone likes to know the manager.

Other sales and promotional items are table tents and lobby posters that announce future events, such as New Year's Eve and Mothers' Day, and dinner/theater combination packages.

Theme nights are very successful in some bars. They give customers an opportunity to participate in the event. Figure 9.5 (p. 130) is a compilation of 70 ideas. Some are straightforward, such as holiday observances; and others require a creative flair and the right setting. But all will stimulate your creative forces and suggest other ideas not named. Consider all of the possibilities associated with themes, contests, prizes, special music, and decorations.

How Do You Want to Be Perceived?

The answer to this question will be the cornerstone of all your advertising, merchandising, sales and promotional, and publicity activities. Once you decide how you want the public to view your business, you must challenge every activity you conduct to be certain it clearly signals your desired image.

Your choice of radio stations and the tone of your commercials, the location of your advertisements in newspapers, the graphic designs and typefaces used, the hard-sell or soft-sell message of your ads, all transmit an image of your business. Advertising budgets typically range from 2% to 3% of sales in the restaurant and bar business (however some are as low as 0% and others as high as 5%).

All employees should have a clear understanding of your desired image and how best to convey it. They are at the point of contact with your customers and can do the most to reinforce your image.

Why Advertise?

Advertising has become a fact of life in the business world. People expect it, look for it, and in spite of many abuses, still place a great deal of trust in it. There are many reasons to advertise bars and restaurants. Here are 15 of the most common reasons.

1. To introduce new entertainment

Figure 9.5:

Special Event and Theme Suggestions

Elvis Night
Labor Day
Back to College Days
Columbus Day
Veteran's Day
Football Day
Thanksgiving Day
Christmas Day
New Year's Day
Super Bowl Day
Homecoming Weekend
Olympics
Mardi Gras
Hockey Games
Basketball Games
Sidewalk Sales
St. Patrick's Day
April Fool's Day
Easter
Mother's Day
Father's Day
Graduation Day
Independence Day
Cajun Night
Washington's Birthday
Lincoln's Birthday
TGIF
Art Exhibit
Patriot's Day
May Day
Dollar Days
Theater Night
Carnival Night
Wine Tastings
Looney Toons Night
Baseball Night

Kentucky Derby
Gay Nineties
Roaring Twenties
Cabaret Night
My Fair Lady
Masked Ball
M*A*S*H Bash
Opera Night
Country Fair
Halloween Party
Marathon Mania
Baby Picture Night
Disco Night
Dance Contest
Salute to the Sixties
Chinese New Year
Jamaican Style Reggae
Hawaiian Cruise
Election Day Party
Down Memory Lane
Bahama Beach Party
Old Time Movie Night
Après Ski
Beatle Mania
Comedy Night
Woodstock Remembered
Platter Party
Sadie Hawkins Night
Mystery Dinner
Chicago 1920s
Soap Opera Night
Sing Along
Fashion Show
Salute to the Armed
    Forces

2. To announce special holiday and theme events

3. To publicize a new or changed menu

4. To position your establishment a certain way

5. To reposition your competition

6. To attract new customers

7. To test new ideas

8. To let the public know what you are doing

9. To resell lost customers

10. To introduce a new management

11. To report achievements to the public

12. To create and maintain a certain image

13. To increase sales

14. To keep your name in the public's eye, particularly if your competitors advertise

15. To engender word-of-mouth advertising

Using Advertising Media Effectively

A great deal of money is wasted on the wrong kind of advertising by businesses desperately seeking to reach new customers. Location and frequency are critical considerations when placing ads. Your ad must run in the proper newspaper or radio or television station. To reach your target market, your ad must air at the right times on the radio and be placed in the right position in the case of newspapers. For example, the inside, lower corner of a newspaper page is a poor location for an ad because many people never see that part of the pages.

The frequency of an ad is also important. The chances of a reader seeing an ad that is run one time is pure luck. But, if the ad is run regularly, the chances are much greater that the reader will see it. In general, it is better to run a smaller size ad more often, than a larger size ad just once. This is especially true with radio advertising, where there is no opportunity to cut out and save a commercial. Figure 9.6 on pages 132 and 133, is a list of types of media, and some of the advantages and disadvantages of each.

Figure 9.6:

Media Analysis

Newspapers

Advantages
- Timely, contain news of the day
- Easy to change on short notice
- Published frequently
- Can tie-in advertisements with local events
- Less expensive than magazines and broadcast media

Disadvantages
- Short life, usually discarded daily
- Ads may get buried among many others
- Some people read certain sections only
- Papers are not as well read on certain days
- Newsprint is not well suited for high quality photos

Magazines

Advantages
- Have a long life, may be saved
- May have multiple readers, are shared, and reread
- May lend prestige to advertiser
- Can be highly targeted to demographic groups, geographic areas, particular lifestyles and special interests
- Better quality paper allows high quality photos

Disadvantages
- Require long lead times up to several months
- May be expensive
- Advertiser may pay for wasted circulation attracted by subscription premiums, rather than real interest

Billboards

Advantages
- Good for reminder ads
- Useful for giving directions

Disadvantages
- Not allowed in certain locations
- Can only accommodate short messages
- Viewership limited mainly to motorists

Car Cards

Advantages
- Most effective in mass transportation vehicles
- Can be located very precisely

Disadvantages
- Viewership limited to riders
- Most useful for short messages or reminder ads

Handbills

Advantages
- Recipient can be targeted easily
- Relatively inexpensive
- May contain coupons, and be saved

Disadvantages
- May create backlash, if they cause littering
- Considered junk mail by some people
- Must be very catchy or they are thrown away

Direct Mail

Advantages
- Can be personalized
- Highly selective; good targeting is possible
- Can be saved or passed on to others
- Computerized mailing lists available
- Can include coupons

Disadvantages
- Very expensive
- Often thrown out as junk mail
- Low percentage of return, usually under 5%

Radio

Advantages
- Easy to target market, through choice of station
- Captive audience during drive times
- 99% of homes are said to have radios
- 95% of all cars are said to have radios

Disadvantages
- Audio only; can't save or cut out
- Lacks visual appeal

Television

Advantages
- Has both audio and visual appeal
- Easy to target market, through choice of program
- Usually no charge for producing the commercial
- Can be heard from another room without viewing

Disadvantages
- Longer time required to produce commercial
- Relatively high cost
- Can't be saved (unless taped)
- Remotes allow muting out of commercials
- VCRs allow fast-forwarding through commercials

Setting Your Sales Goals

There are many approaches to setting sales goals, but the best is to use a combination of several methods and temper it with your own gut feeling. Industry sources, such as the National Restaurant Association's *Annual Restaurant Operations Report* can give you typical sales figures for various types of establishments. The figures are expressed in total dollar amounts as well as sales per seat. Trade journals also conduct surveys and publish their results. These are all good numbers to use as cross references, but you should calculate your own numbers based on your seating capacity, expected turnovers meal-by-meal and day-by-day, and average guest check amount.

Step 1: Estimate the number of customers you might expect during each meal period, for each day of the week.

No. of Customers Expected Per Week
(sum of daily estimates)

	Total
Lunch	573
Dinner	417
Bar Only	205
Total Customers per Week	*1,195*

Step 2: Calculate the average menu price for each category of items on your menu. (A weighted average method, which takes into account the popularity and sales of each item, is a more refined method, but until you are in business for a while and have a track record, this simple average method will suffice.)

Average Menu Prices

Sandwiches and Salads	$4.95
Entrees	8.95
Desserts	2.75
Drinks	2.75

Step 3: Determine the amount of an average guest check by estimating what the typical guest will order. If you expect that only one out of every

two guests will order an item, you may count it fractionally. This will keep your estimate on the conservative side.

Estimated Average Guest Check Per Person

Lunch	Sandwich or Salad plus Drink	$ 6.35
Dinner	Entree, Salad, Dessert, plus Drinks	22.79
Bar Only	Average 2 Drinks	5.50

Step 4: Multiply your average guest check by the number of customers expected per week to determine your estimated weekly sales.

Estimated Weekly Sales

573 customers	x	$ 6.35	=	$3,638
417 customers	x	22.79	=	9,504
205 customers	x	5.50	=	1,127
Total Weekly Sales				$14,269

Step 5: Finally, multiply your estimated weekly sales by 52 to arrive at your estimated annual sales.

Estimated Annual Sales

52 weeks	x	$14,629	=	$760,716

This process tailors your sales objective to your specific business and local conditions. The resultant annual sales figure may be compared to industry averages. Figure 9.7 (p. 137) describes some tips for achieving your goals.

Don't Overlook Telephone Selling

A telephone sales blitz is an excellent way to notify the business community of your function rooms and group packages. Telephone calls are less costly and faster to make than personal visits. You can solicit a variety of bookings—such as retirement parties, holiday and birthday parties, promotion parties, sales meetings, and awards presentation meetings. Calls work best when followed up with a sales packet and a letter which reviews the content of the call.

A significant amount of interest in your establishment can be raised with a carefully planned and tested telephone message. A telephone script should contain all of the basic elements of a personal sales call, namely

- a brief introduction that tells the listener who you are and the purpose of your call,
- an attention getting statement that gives the listener a reason for continuing to listen,
- a discussion of the features and benefits of your offering,

---

Figure 9.7:

Sales Tips

1. Maintain a positive attitude. All months are not created equal. There will be slow times. You can offset slow periods to some degree by being creative and coming up with ideas that "keep smoke in the chimneys," but your main focus should be on maximizing your sales when people feel like coming out and are ready to spend money.

2. Be prepared. That is the secret to maximizing sales. Take advantage of the opportunities when they are there. Be ready to handle a crowd.

3. Believe in yourself. It has been said in fiction, "If you build it, they will come." In the public hospitality business, it can be said, "As long as you give your customers what they want, they will keep coming back." Set high standards, serve good drinks, keep your establishment clean and attractive, offer a good value and you will soon get valuable word of mouth advertising from your present customers.

4. Establish a rapport with your customers. Let them know you care about them. That way, if you have to shut them off some night, they will not be resentful toward you.

5. Listen to your customers. Hear their compliments and their complaints. They are telling you what they like and don't like.

6. Never embarrass a customer for mispronouncing the name of a wine or a menu item. Be sympathetic and helpful. Try to build customers up, not diminish them in any way.

- an opportunity for the listener to ask questions or voice any objections, and

- an appeal for an action of some sort or a subsequent meeting.

Your Menu is a Powerful Selling Tool

Menus have three basic purposes. One is to let customers know what you offer, and the second is to let them know how much things cost. The third and less obvious, purpose is to promote the sale of certain, highly profitable, items.

Sales may be enhanced by bringing certain items to the attention of customers. Boxing an item makes it stand out on a menu as shown in Figure 9.8.

Studies have shown that eyes tend to follow certain patterns, depicted in Figure 9.9 (p. 138), when reading menus. Knowing this, you can place items you want to promote in strategic locations.

Figure 9.8: Boxed Menu Item

How a Wine List Sells

Wines will sell much better if they are promoted, and your wine list is your best sales promotion tool. A good wine list should not be so long as

3rd spot	MENU	2nd spot
	First spot to be seen	
4th spot		Last spot

Figure 9.9: How Customers Tend to See Your Menu.

to be confusing, but it should have enough choices to be interesting. It should provide adequate complement to your food menu. Be sure to include the items that are popular in your area.

When designing a wine list, choose descriptive words that are easy to understand. Avoid vague expressions, like "it has excellent nose and a lasting taste that challenges the palate." Also shun snobbish words that may send inappropriate messages to inexperienced wine drinkers. Try to use positive words that will enhance the appeal of your wines and assist your customers in matching them with food items. Operate on the premise that all your wines are good, it's just that some are better with certain foods. If a wine is not good, you should not carry it.

Check your wine inventory turnover periodically to weed out the slow movers. It is good to search out new wines that your customers might enjoy but do not make your bar a testing ground for every new product. In general, stay with tried and proven brands.

A logical order for posting wines on your wine list is 1) before dinner wines, 2) red dinner wines, 3) white dinner wines, 4) sparkling wines, and 5) after dinner wines. Wine lists should be printed on substantial stock so as not to quickly wear, or become dog-eared. Your name should appear prominently on all wine lists. As with menus, your design can promote certain wines through boxing their names or highlighting with a special style of print or color.

Ways to Increase Wine Sales

Wait staff should be trained to present wine lists before guests order their food and to suggestively sell wines, in a helpful manner. It should be noted that wine sales are truly an add-on sale, since the alternative beverage a customer is most apt to choose is water.

Some helpful hints on making wine lists easy for customers to use are:

- Assign bin numbers to each wine, giving customers the opportunity to order by number if they cannot pronounce the name of the wine.

- Use large type sizes, which make wines seem less intimidating to inexperienced wine drinkers and assists people with visual impairments.

- Print wine lists on white or very light colored stock for easy reading. The covers of a wine menu should coordinate with the colors of the decor and the mood of the atmosphere.

- Use descriptions that clearly describe a wine and suggest foods that will go well with it or vice versa.

- Select a wine list size that is appropriate to your table sizes. Oversized and odd shaped wine lists can monopolize a tabletop and be a nuisance to guests.

- Proofread wine lists carefully before approving them for printing. Especially when foreign names and terms are used.

Some establishments have incentive plans to stimulate wait staff to suggest wines to guests before they order food. Table tents and menu clip-ons can sometimes be used to promote a particular type of wine. It is a good idea to post a wine chart near the servers' pick up station at the bar (but out of guests' sight) for quick, easy reference.

Pricing—A Marketing Tool

The prices a bar charges will influence the type of clientele it attracts. Higher prices are usually associated with entertainment, a special location, or ambiance. Management should constantly challenge its prices, to assure that they are appropriate to the style of service and the quality and quantity of the products served, as well as in line with competitors' prices for comparable offerings. At any level of pricing, the customer must perceive value commensurate with the prices they are paying.

People tend to be less forgiving of poor quality products or service when higher prices are charged. There are few second chances given in the food and beverage business. Customers simply do not return when dissatisfied, and what is worse, they tell their friends about their poor experience.

Pricing Mixed Drinks

There are a number of ways to price drinks. Some are simple, and others are more complicated. All of them are acceptable as long as they cover costs and expenses, yield a desired level of profit, and are perceived by customers as being worth the value of the product they receive. Following is one method for pricing drinks:

Assume:
 a) a liter of whiskey costs $7.20.

 b) drink prices are based on a 20% pouring cost. (That means 20% of the price of a drink goes to pay for its ingredients.)

 c) your standard pour is 1.5 ounces. (A pour is the amount of alcohol you put into a standard drink.)

 d) you allow 1.8 ounces out of every bottle, for spillage. 33.8 oz.–1.8 oz. = 32 salable ounces (21.3 pours of 1.5 oz. each).

Step 1: Cost of Bottle ÷ Pouring Cost % = Sales Yield
$7.20 ÷ .20 = $36 (sales yield of bottle)

Step 2: Sales Yield ÷ No. of Pours = Selling Price
$36 ÷ 21.3 = $1.69 (selling price of drink)

Step 3: Add a "kicker" of 25¢ to 50¢ to cover the cost of garnishes and mixers. The selling price may be further adjusted to defray entertainment costs and other special considerations, such as an unusually high rent in a seasonal location.

Using the above method, the example drink would probably sell for $2.25. If larger drinks, or drinks requiring more liquors, were served the same pricing system could be used and, a higher selling price would result.

Prior to the advent of computerized cash registers, bar owners were concerned that bartenders would not be able to remember a great many prices, and felt that mistakes would more than offset the benefits of pricing drinks individually. Consequently, a tiered pricing system was frequently used. Under the tiered system, all drinks that were made with one liquor would have one average price, all two liquor drinks would have another, higher, average price, and so on for three liquor drinks.

Today, cash registers can be programmed to handle as many drink prices as a bar wants to serve, and they are easy for bartenders to use—the bartender simply presses the key bearing the name of the drink. There is nothing to remember. They will even tell the bartender how much change to give the customer from the amount tendered.

Pricing Wines

The philosophy for pricing wines has always been different than that of mixed drinks. Partly because wines are often bought by the bottle and therefore command higher prices, and because they are considered add-on sales. It has always been considered best to use a flexible markup system, whereby higher cost wines are priced for resale with a smaller percentage of markup. This method of pricing makes better wines more affordable and increases their sales. For example,

Wine A—costs $8.50 per bottle. It is priced with a 100% markup to sell at $17. Gross profit per bottle = $8.50.

Wine B—costs $26 per bottle. It is priced with a 50% markup to sell at $39. Gross profit per bottle = $11.00.

In the above example, the establishment will earn an additional $2.50 of gross profit, when they sell a bottle of wine B. In addition, more good wines will sell because many customers will recognize their greater relative value.

Pricing Beer

Three main factors determine the selling price of draught (pronounced draft) beer . They are the cost of the beer, the size of the beer glass, and the size of the head poured. As with other beverages the final selling price will be influenced by the bar cost percentage desired, and the cost of entertainment or an unusually high rent. In general, however, the selling prices of draught beer is calculated as follows:

Assume:	Half barrel keg costs	$50
	Keg contains	1,980 oz.
		(approximately)
	Cost per ounce	$0.025
	Cost per 13 oz. hour glass, which actually holds about 10.4 oz. of beer (assuming a one inch head is poured)	$0.26
	Marked up 5 times, to accommodate a desired 20% bar cost percentage	$1.31
	(Selling price rounded to $1.30)	

Following is an illustration of how to calculate the profit potential of a keg of beer. (Assume a one inch head of foam per glass.)

Size of glass used (13 ounce hour glass)	13 oz.
No. of glasses in a half barrel (keg)	190
Price per glass	$1.30
Total sales value of a half barrel keg (190 x $1.30)	$247
Less: Cost of half barrel keg	$50
PROFIT	$197

In the above example, the bar is selling beer at a very profitable 21% pouring cost and its price is competitive. The four keys to selling a lot of beer are to 1) carry the brands your customers want, 2) keep your beer stored at the proper temperature (38° - 42° F.) and gauge pressure (12-14 psi), 3) keep your dispensing system meticulously clean, and 4) price your beers competitively.

The recent popularity of premium micro-brewery beers cannot be overlooked. Many discriminating beer drinkers are willing to pay substantially more for a bottle of their favorite premium beer, provided they can take their time drinking it in a pleasant atmosphere. As with other beers, the key to selling a lot of premium beers is to know the brands your customers want and carry them. Micro-brewed beers cost more at wholesale, but command a higher price at retail, and therefore can be very profitable.

Entertainment Surcharge

One way to calculate an entertainment surcharge is shown below. It spreads the cost of entertainment over the average number of drinks served on nights when entertainment is offered.

Step 1:

$$\frac{\text{Entertainment Cost per Night}}{\text{Average No. of Drinks Sold per Night}} = \text{Entertainment Surcharge}$$

$$\frac{\$450}{600} = \$.75$$

Step 2:

	Basic Price of Drink	$3.00
+	Entertainment Surcharge	+ $ .75
	Adjusted Selling Price of Drink	$3.75

Action Guidelines

✔ Develop a seven step marketing plan for a new bar.

✔ Describe in a detailed paragraph the identifying characteristics of your target market

✔ Write a press release announcing the grand opening of your bar.

✔ Create a beverage menu that includes wines, beers, and spirits.

✔ Calculate the selling prices of a 5 oz. glass of table wine, a 12 oz. glass of draft beer, and a highball made with 1.25 oz. of bar whiskey.

✔ Plan an advertising campaign, based on 3% of your estimated sales, allocating the funds among the media you select.

✔ Make a list of the people you would invite to your pre-opening party.

KNOW YOUR PRODUCTS

I n the course of starting and operating an alcoholic beverage establishment, you will need to buy an initial inventory of wines, beers,
and spirits that will satisfy your clientele. You will also need to replen-
ish that supply weekly. Beyond that, you will often be asked to recommend a wine to a customer, and you may wish to offer wine tastings in
your establishment. As a professional in the hospitality field, you may on
occasion be invited to speak to a club on wines or liquors.

To do these things, you must have at least a working knowledge of the
many products available. You should be able to discern their differences
and be able to discuss them confidently. In this chapter you will find the
basic information on wines, beers, spirits, and liqueurs that will allow you
to do that.

Wines

There are five general types of wines. Since wine is usually consumed with
a meal, they are shown in Figure 10.1, on p. 146, as they relate to the various parts of a meal.

Which Wine with Which Food

Most people believe the flavors of red dinner wines complement the flavor of red meats, particularly steaks and roast beef. White dinner wines
are usually found to go best with light meals, such as veal, fish, and fowl,

Type of Wine	Examples
1. Appetizer Wines	Dry Sherry, Vermouth
2. Dinner Wines	
Red	Burgundy, Chianti, Cabernet Sauvignon, Beaujolais
White	Chablis, Chardonnay, Liebfraumilch, Pouilly Fuissé
3. Dessert Wines	Port, Cream Sherry, Muscatel
4. Sparkling Wines	Champagne, Cold Duck, Sparkling Burgundy
5. Blush and Rosé Wines	White Zinfandel, Rosé

Figure 10.1: Wine Types.

because the clean, light taste of white wines does not overpower the delicate flavors of those meats. Rosés, Champagnes, and other sparkling wines go well with all types of food, and are excellent as appetizer and dessert wines as well.

Always be guided by the principle that customers are entitled to their own preferences and above all, never embarrass customers for their lack of knowledge about wine or their poor pronunciation of a name.

Storing Wines

Only wine bottles with corks need to be stored on their sides. This prevents the cork from drying and becoming porous and brittle. Bottles with plastic or metal caps can be stored upright. The ideal temperature for a storeroom is about 60° F.

Serving Wines

Red dinner wines should be served at cool room temperatures, 55° to 65° F. White wine should be refrigerated and served at about 45° F.

Premium red wines will develop a fuller aroma if opened and left to stand uncapped for about 45 minutes before service. This is not practical to do in busy bars, but it is possible in banquet wine service. Some wine experts contend that merely uncorking the bottle does little to develop the wine, citing that the most effective way to achieve the desired result is to decant wines.

How to Open Wine Bottles

Champagne—tilt the bottle, and while grasping the cork firmly with one hand, slowly turn the bottle with your other hand. The cork will start to come out very slightly after three or four turns. After a few more turns it will come out completely without the champagne gushing.

Corked Still Wines—insert the auger of a corkscrew straight into middle of cork, as far down as it will go, then pull the cork out slowly and steadily. Smell the cork to be sure it has not become pungent, and check the cork for damage.

How Much Wine to Serve

Appetizer and dessert wines have a greater alcoholic content than do dinner and sparkling wines, therefore smaller portions of those wines are served. Three ounces is generally considered adequate.

Dinner wines are considered part of a meal, because they are consumed with food. Four to five ounces (depending on the glass size) is considered an appropriate portion.

Figure 10.2: The wine cellars of Schramsberg Vineyards and Cellars, in Calistoga, CA. (Photo courtesy of Schramsberg Vineyards.)

Sparkling wines, if served with food, are treated like dinner wines (4 to 5 oz.), but if served before or after the meal are treated like appetizer or dessert wines (3 oz.).

How to Judge Wine

There are several instances when a bar manager will need to know how to judge wines—when buying them, when a customer complains about a wine not being good, and when conducting wine tastings.

Three factors are most often used to evaluate wines: color, aroma, and taste.

The color of a wine should be clear and shiny, regardless of whether it is a red or white wine. Any wine that appears dull or cloudy is inferior. The color of a wine may be checked by viewing it through a glass held up to a light.

The aroma of a good wine should be pleasing, not overwhelming and never pungent. It should be faint, yet noticeable enough to be exciting.

Finally, the taste should be engaging to the palate. Some wines are intended to be sweet, and others dry. Sweet and dry are relative terms, with dry referring to the lack of sweetness. See Figure 10.3.

A good wine should always have a satisfying taste, given its own characteristics. Signs of poor wines are vinegar-like flavors, an unclear appearance, and a strong or unpleasant aroma.

How Are Wines Named?

Some wines are named after the region where they are produced. These are called *generic* names. Some examples of generically named wines are Burgundy, Rhine, Bordeaux, and Concord. Other wines are named after the variety of the principal grape from which they are made. Those are called *varietal* names. Examples of varietal names are Cabernet Sauvignon, Pinot Noir, Chardonnay, and Catawba.

The choice of a name is usually decided by the relative popularity of each option. If the region is more highly acclaimed, that is the name the producer will most likely choose. If the grape variety is the most prestigious, that is what the producer will use. Wines may also be given proprietary names if they would have market value. There are controls associated with the production of wines bearing certain names. To be able to use those names, producers must adhere to strict regulations.

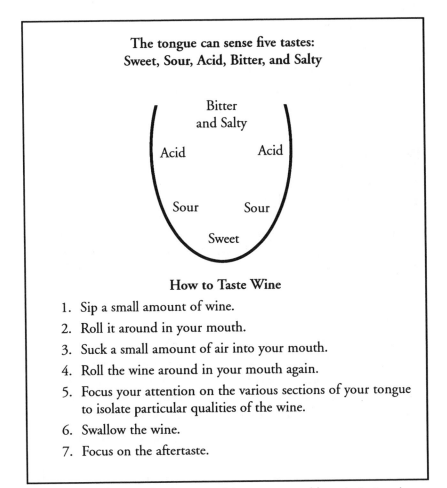

**The tongue can sense five tastes:
Sweet, Sour, Acid, Bitter, and Salty**

Bitter
and Salty

Acid   Acid

Sour   Sour

Sweet

How to Taste Wine

1. Sip a small amount of wine.

2. Roll it around in your mouth.

3. Suck a small amount of air into your mouth.

4. Roll the wine around in your mouth again.

5. Focus your attention on the various sections of your tongue to isolate particular qualities of the wine.

6. Swallow the wine.

7. Focus on the aftertaste.

Figure 10.3: The taste bud zones of the tongue and how to taste wine.

How to Read a Wine Label

Information on a label can be very helpful when selecting wines. To better understand a wine, the following list of items should be checked.

- The name of the wine—varietal or generic

- The country or place of origin

- The type of grape from which it is made

- The size of the bottle
- The percentage of alcohol content
- The vintage date, if applicable
- The shipper's or importer's name, if it is an imported wine
- Any official statements that guarantee the authenticity of the wine

Beer and Ale

Beer has been enjoyed by mankind for thousands of years. References to beer were found inscribed on Babylonian tablets, more than 6,000 years old. Beer also played an important role in the societies of the ancient Greeks, Romans, and Hebrews, as well as the Teutonic tribes of Europe. Beer came to America on the *Mayflower,* the diary of one pilgrim reveals. Whatever its origin was in the New World, it has since become America's top selling alcoholic beverage.

Types of Beers and Ale

For many years, Americans focused mainly on two malt beverages, lager beer and ale. Today, however, with the new interest in boutique or micro-brewed beers and ales, there is a realization that there are numerous types of beer and ale, each with its own characteristics and special appeal. Following is a list of terms that apply to the more common beers and ales:

- **Beer:** an alcoholic beverage obtained by the fermentation of a malted grain to which hops have been added for seasoning.
- **Lager Beer:** any beer made by the bottom-fermentation method, that is stored under refrigeration for maturing and clarification. Most American beers are lager beers.
- **Bock Beer:** a strong beer that is heavy, dark, and rich; produced by the bottom-fermentation method. Often prepared for consumption in spring.
- **Ale:** a pale bright colored beverage, made with a top-fermenting yeast that gives it a distinctive taste with a pronounced hop character and a more tart taste than beer.
- **Porter:** made like ale by the top-fermentation method. Heavier and darker than ale, but lighter than stout. Less hop flavor and sweeter in taste.

- **Stout:** an extra dark brew made by the top-fermentation method; has a strong malt flavor, is made like ale and porter, but heavier than porter.

- **Malt Liquor:** made like beer, but has a fruity and spicy flavor and a higher alcoholic content than regular beer.

- **Dark Beer:** made like regular lager beer, but has a dark color (obtained from a darker toasted malt). Not as sweet as bock beer.

- **Pilsner:** inspired by the original brew from the town of Pilsen in Czechoslovakia. Refers to any conventional, golden colored, dry beer made by the bottom-fermentation method. Has a light, hoppy flavor.

Rules for Proper Beer Handling

Beer drinkers expect a good beer every time they order one. It is not difficult to serve good beer, provided the dispensing equipment is kept clean and in good operating condition, and the beer is handled properly. Following are a few simple rules, which if adhered to will allow you to serve a good beer every time:

- Keep beer fresh. Whenever new beer arrives, pull the older beer out to the front and place the new beer in the rear. This assures the older stock will get used first.

- Store bottled and canned beer in a cool, dark, and dry place.

- Avoid exposing beer to freezing temperatures.

- Store kegged beer at 38° F. This allows it to be served at about 40° F. in a glass. Chilled mugs or glasses are always desirable.

- Serve beer in clean glasses. Any residual soap or oily film on glasses causes beer to go flat.

- Put keg beer into refrigeration immediately after delivery.

Bartenders should be trained to solve beer problems. If regular maintenance is performed on equipment, and the dispensing system is cleaned on a regular schedule, there should be a minimum of problems related to beer. Nevertheless, bartenders should be acquainted with the information in Figure 10.4 (p. 152).

If Your Problem is:	Then a Possible Cause is:
Flat Beer	• Greasy glasses • CO_2 pressure not turned on
Loose Foam	• Drawing too short a head • Not drawing beer properly • Flat beer causes (see above)
Cloudy Beer	• Bottled or canned beer was kept too warm at some time or other • Beer is old • Tap lines are dirty; need flushing
Wild Beer	• Improper drawing of beer • Beer kept too warm in package or in tap lines • Creeping pressure gauges (increasing pressure)
Off-Tasting Beer	• Glasses not clean • Lines not clean • Beer too warm
Sour Beer	• Quite possible the keg was not kept properly refrigerated. The temperature of keg beer should never be allowed to rise over 50° F.

Figure 10.4: Potential problems in beer.

Brew Pubs and Micro-Breweries

A brew pub is a broad term used to describe establishments that make and sell beer for consumption on the premises. Some purists say a true brew pub just makes and sells beer, nothing else. Consequently, new terms are emerging that more precisely describe the nature of establishments that make their own beer but also engage in other activities, namely restaurant breweries and brewery inns.

Chart of Beer Glasses and Yields

	Heavy Base Pilsner	Hour Glass Pilsner	Pilsner	Mug	Shell	Goblet
Approximate Number of Glasses per 1/2 Barrel of Beer						
10 Oz. Glass	264	248	248	256	248	283
12 Oz. Glass	198	214	208	198	198	240

Figure 10.5: Here are some of the more popular types of glassware in two common sizes and the approximate yield that may be obtained from a half barrel of beer, assuming each glass is properly poured and has a one inch head of foam. Specifications for all glasses may be obtained from most beer distributors.

Figure 10.6: Brewer, Paul Murphy and an assistant prepare to make a batch of beer at the Portsmouth Brewery, in Portsmouth, NH. (Photo supplied by Portsmouth Brewery.)

A micro-brewery is generally considered to be a small brewery with proprietary recipes and an annual production of not more than 15,000 to 20,000 barrels of beer. Craft breweries are makers of small batches of specialized beers that are marketed through regular channels of distribution. With names like Smuttynose Brewery, they capture the imagination and strike the fancy of true beer drinkers. Each brand has its small, but loyal following.

Micro-breweries, though minute by comparison to the major breweries, have caught the eye of the large breweries. Some major breweries are even developing their own micro-breweries, that will function as small, independent entities within the larger organization.

Although micro-brewed beers are still less than 1% of all beer sold in this country, there are close to 400 micro-breweries and brew pubs as of 1994 and that number is growing rapidly.

Distilled Spirits

A spirit is an alcoholic beverage that is derived from the distillation of a fermented mash of grain or a wine. Some distilled spirits are aged in wood to develop their body and flavor, while others are bottled immediately. Unlike wines, spirits do not continue to improve after they have been bottled.

Although the basic principle of distillation has not changed since an Arabic alchemist is said to have discovered it in the 11th century, a great many differences in liquors have emerged over the years with varying the ingredients, production, and aging techniques. The main categories of distilled spirits and the products from which they are derived are shown in Figure 10.7.

Each category of distilled spirits has subdivisions that vary according to taste and age. Whiskey, for example, includes Scotch, Bourbon, Irish, Canadian, Tennessee, Corn, Rye, and blended whiskies. The name whiskey (spelled whisky in Scotland and Canada) stems from the Celtic name for a distilled spirit, uisgebaugh. Although the art of distilling was discovered many centuries ago, spirits of the quality we know today, are much more recent.

The most common grains used in the production of spirits are wheat, corn, rye, and barley; but any fermentable food product can be distilled

---

Figure 10.7:

Distilled Spirits

Type of Spirit	Distinctive Ingredient from which it is Made
Whiskey	Grains: wheat, corn, rye, barley
Brandy	Distilled wine
Gin	Neutral grain spirits (flavored with Juniper berries and other herbs and spices)
Vodka	Neutral grain spirits
Tequila	Juice of the heart of the mescal plant
Rum	Sugarcane molasses

to produce a spirituous beverage. When a spirit is distilled to 190 proof or more it is called a *neutral spirit* because it has lost virtually all characteristic color, flavor, and aroma reminiscent of the product from which it was made.

When the prohibition era ended in 1933, the federal government developed specific definitions for every type of liquor. The definitions specify the ingredients that must be used, both the type and proportion, and the percentage of alcohol at the time of distilling and at the time of bottling.

Federal laws govern the names and claims that can be given to alcoholic beverages. Rye whiskey, for example, must have at least 51% rye in its mash. Bourbon must be produced from a mash of at least 51% corn. Whiskies cannot be identified as Bourbon or rye if they are distilled at over 160 proof.

Relationship of Proof to Percentage of Alcohol

Proof is a term given to the measurement of alcohol in a distillate. The term is said to have come from the days when whiskey makers would test the readiness of their liquor by pouring some on a small amount of gun powder and lighting it. If it did not burn, it was said to be underproof (not ready yet) because it did not contain enough alcohol. If it ignited with a flash, it was said to be overproof (containing too much alcohol) and needed to be aged more or watered down to a drinkable state. Finally, if it burned with a steady glow, it was considered to be just right, and had "proved" it was fit to drink.

The relationship of *proof* to *percentage of alcohol* is two to one. Put another way, percentage is one-half of proof. A 100° proof whiskey, would therefore contain 50 percent alcohol, just as a liquor with 40 percent alcohol would be 80 proof.

What Does Bottled in Bond Mean?

If a distilled spirit meets certain government requirements, it may be stamped *bottled in bond.* The stamp is not a guarantee of quality, it merely assures that the product conforms to certain United States Treasury Department requirements.

The requirements for whiskey state that it must be a straight whiskey, at least four years old, distilled at one plant, bottled at 100 proof, and secured in a U.S. Treasury Department supervised warehouse. Other distilled spirits may also be stamped bottled in bond provided they meet specific U.S. Treasury Department requirements. The bottled in bond stamp has less significance today, since straight whiskeys are usually aged in bonded warehouses for well over four years.

Common Spirits

Straight Whiskies versus Blended Whiskies. A straight whiskey is one that has been distilled at not over 160 proof, from a fermented mash of a least 51 percent of the grain for which it is named (rye or corn) and has been aged in charred, new oak barrels for at least two years.

A blended whiskey must contain at least 20 percent of a straight whiskey. The remainder may be neutral grain spirits and or other whiskies selected for their blending qualities. In addition, up to 2.5 percent special blending materials, such as sherry blending wine, may be included.

Canadian Whiskey. By law, this must be a blend of whiskies that have been distilled in Canada from cereal grains (corn is preferred because of its high starch content and ease of sugar conversion; but rye, wheat, and barley malt are also used). It must be aged at least two years. However, most Canadian whiskies are actually aged six or more years. If any are aged fewer than four years, they must be so described on the label. Canadian whisky is marketed at 80 to 100 proof levels.

Scotch Whiskey. Two things in particular give Scotch whisky its characteristic flavor; 1) the influence of the smoke from the peat moss fires used in malting the barley grains, and 2) the very clear tasting waters found in the Scottish Highlands. By international agreement, Scotch whiskey must be distilled in Scotland (but, it may be bottled in any country). It must be aged for at least three years.

Scotch whiskies may be single-malt whiskies or blended whiskies. Single-malt whiskies must be produced from a single barley malt at a single distillery. Blended whiskies may be mixtures of as many as thirty different malt and grain whiskies. The vast majority of Scotch whiskies are blended.

A significant amount of barreled Scotch whisky is exported in barrels to the United States at high proofs. Upon arrival its proof is reduced through the addition of water and it is bottled for sale under a domestic label. This is done for tax saving reasons, since taxes on imported spirits are based on the "proof gallon." Most Scotch whiskies are reduced to 80 to 86 proof in the United States.

Scotch whiskies that are bottled in Scotland command higher prices than do those bottled in the United States. Part of the higher prices can be attributed to greater shipping costs. Distillers in Scotland further justify the higher prices with the contention that the waters from the Highland rivers and streams give their Scotch whiskey a special character that cannot be duplicated anywhere else.

Irish Whiskey. Most Irish whiskies are blended grain whiskies. They are produced much like Scotch whiskies, except that in the malting process smoke is not allowed contact with the sprouted barley as it dries. This gives the final product a different taste than Scotch whiskey. Another difference is that Irish whiskey is distilled three times. This contributes to a noticeable smoothness to the product. It is usually marketed at 80 proof in the United States.

Bourbon Whiskey. Bourbon whiskey was named after Bourbon County, Kentucky, and Kentuckians take immense pride in its waters which run through the great limestone shelf underlying their state as well as Tennessee and Indiana. The limestone imparts a distinctive quality to the waters.

America's popular contribution to the world of spirits enjoys an international reputation. Bourbon is produced at 160 proof or less, from a fermented mash of at least 51 percent corn, and is stored at not more than 125 proof in new, charred, oak barrels.

Two yeasting processes are used in the production of American whiskies—the *sweet mash* process and the *sour mash* process. Sweet mash is produced by adding freshly cultured yeast to the mash during the fermentation stage. Sour mash is produced by adding a portion of the previous fermentation to the new mash, along with a new yeast. Bourbon is made by the sour mash process and is bottled at 80 to over 100 proof.

Tennessee Whiskey. In spite of its similarities with the Bourbon production process, Tennessee whiskey has its own distinctive taste and reputation.

An important step in the production of some Tennessee whiskies, credited for its unique flavor, is filtering it through vats of ground and tightly compacted charcoal, up to 12 feet deep.

The charcoal comes from local hard maple trees cut after the sap runs and is then burned under control at the distillery. It takes 10 or more days for the distillate to completely pass through the bed of charcoal. The filtering process, which immediately follows distillation, enhances the whiskey's flavor. Tennessee whisky is often referred to as a sipping whiskey and is bottled at 80 to more than 100 proof.

Gin. Today, two basic categories of gin are produced—Hollands gin and dry gin. The two have extremely different tastes. Hollands gin has a flavor reminiscent of whiskey, due to the lower proof at which it is distilled. It is not very popular in the United States. Dry gin is by far the most popular. It is made from neutral grain spirits which have no characteristic grain flavor of their own, but are flavored by botanical additives.

Dry gin is a clear beverage, usually bottled at 80 to 95 proof. Since it does not require aging, it is usually bottled shortly after production. If it is to be held in storage for a while, it is kept in glass-lined containers where it cannot acquire a woody taste. Dry gins produced in the British Isles tend to be of slightly lower proof.

Fruit flavored gins (such as lime, orange, and lemon) maintain a small market in the United States. These products have distinctive tastes and cannot be used as substitutes for regular gin. They must be clearly labeled as to their flavor.

Vodka. Vodka is defined as a neutral spirit without character, taste, or aroma. In the past decade, vodka has enjoyed the fastest growing sales of any distilled spirit in the United States. Its lack of character, taste, and aroma make it an ideal accompaniment for liqueurs, juices, soft drinks, and milk or cream products in mixed drinks.

Grain is the most commonly used product for making vodka, but it may be produced from a variety of fermentable sources including potatoes. Most vodkas marketed in the United States are bottled in the 80° to 100° proof range.

A growing number of flavored vodkas have appeared on the market in recent years. They have delightful qualities of their own, but cannot be used as substitutes, generally, in drink recipes that call for regular vodka.

Rum. Rum is an alcoholic distillate obtained from the fermented juice of sugarcane, or its molasses. The first commercial rum in the colonies was distilled in Massachusetts in 1670 with molasses imported from the West Indies.

Today, the most common distinctions among rums in the American marketplace are: white or light rum, golden or medium rum, and dark or heavy rum. So-called white rums are colorless and have gained popularity as ingredients in mixed drinks because they have a dry, light taste with only a slight suggestion of molasses. Medium rums have a golden color resulting from their longer aging in oak barrels and the addition of a small amount of caramel. Dark rums are distilled at lower proofs and as a result have a heavy concentration of congeners, which give them a full bodied taste of molasses. The mahogany color of dark rum is acquired by the addition of caramel. Most rums are bottled at 80° proof, but some rums are bottled at as high as 151 proof.

Tequila. Tequila is Mexico's famous spirit. Its origins extend as far back as the pre-Columbian culture of the Aztec Indians. It is a distillate derived from the juice of the mescal plant, which is a species of the agave plant.

Most Tequila is bottled immediately in Mexico, because it does not require aging. However, a small amount of golden tequila is aged. Most tequilas are marketed at 80° proof in the United States.

Brandy. The development of brandy is said to have occurred accidentally. An enterprising Flemish ship master, seeking to increase the amount of wine he could carry on his vessel, concentrated his wines by evaporating them, with the intention of adding water back to the wine at its destination point. As it turned out, the concentrated product was received with such enthusiasm when it was tasted on arrival, that no effort was made to add the water back. The new product was called by its Dutch name, *brandewijn*, which means burnt wine. The name gradually evolved to the shorter, anglicized *brandy.*

Brandy is the distillate of wine. Since wines can be fermented from a wide variety of fruits, brandies can be distilled from many kinds of wine. The most popular brandy in the world is France's cognac. However, a number of other countries produce fine brandies.

It should be noted that all cognacs are brandies, but very few brandies are cognacs. Only those brandies produced according to strict legal regulations, within the departments of Charente and Charente-Maritime in southern France, may be called Cognac. The town of Cognac is located within that region and gives these brandies their famous name.

All Cognacs are blended. The exceptional ones are not blended until later, but others may be blended as early as the first year. Today most cognacs are given one of two broad classifications:

- *3 Star:* More than 80 percent of them aged three to five years before bottling

- *V.S.O.P.:* Means *Very Superior Old Pale.* These cognacs are aged an average of seven to ten years.

The uniform coloring of cognac is achieved by the addition of caramel. Before bottling, cognac is brought down to 80° to 86° proof by the addition of distilled water. In order to allow the cognac time to marry its blends and additives, bottling is not done for many months after.

Cognac continues to improve in oak casks for many years, but once it is bottled, the enhancement process ceases. It has long been said, the best age for cognac is 20 to 40 years, but today very few cognacs reach that age. The high cost of keeping them in inventory and the significant loss that occurs over time through evaporation in the cask, make lengthy aging uneconomical.

Brandies. Most of the brandy production in the United States is located in California, where the Thompson Seedless grape is the main species used to make brandy. American brandies should not be compared to cognac—they are quite different products. But, if evaluated on their own merits, and in terms of the markets for which they are produced, most fare quite well.

Fruit Brandies. The fermented mash of fruits and berries may be distilled to make fruit brandies. Following is a list of some of the better known fruit brandies and their sources:

- Applejack—Apples
- Calvados—Apples
- Apricot Brandy—Apricots
- Blackberry Brandy—Blackberries
- Kirsch—Cherry
- Elderberry Brandy—Elderberries
- Framboise—Raspberries
- Fraise—Strawberries

Unaged fruit brandies are colorless. The golden hue of some fruit brandies is the result of aging in wood. Color is also enhanced, in some instances, by the addition of fruit juice.

Liqueurs and Cordials. The words *liqueur* and *cordial* are used interchangeably. The base spirits for virtually all liqueurs are neutral grain spir-

Figure 10.8:

Liqueur Flavors

Name of Liqueur	Flavor
Advocaat	Eggnog
Amaretto	Almond
Amer Picon	Bitter orange
Anisette	Anise, licorice
Apple Jack	Apple
Benedictine	Cognac base, unique concoction of flavoring agents
B & B	Mixture of brandy & benedictine
Chambord	Raspberry
Chartreuse	Unique concoction of flavoring agents
Cherry Heering	Cherry
Cointreau	Bitter orange
Creme de Almond (Noyaux)	Bitter almond
Creme de Ananas	Pineapple
Creme de Bananas	Banana
Creme de Cacao	Chocolate, vanilla
Creme de Cassis	Black currants
Creme de Framboise	Raspberry
Creme de Menthe	Mint leaves
Creme de Vanilla	Vanilla
Creme de Yvette	Violets
Curacao	Bitter orange
Drambuie	Honey & Scotch whiskey
Forbidden Fruit	Sweet, citrus
Frangelica	Hazelnut
Galliano	Licorice, vanilla, sweet citrus
Grand Marnier	Brandy, orange
Irish Mist	Honey & Irish whiskey
Kahlua	Sweet black coffee syrup
Kummel	Caraway
Midori	Honeydew melon
Ouzo	Anise, licorice
Peppermint Schnapps	Peppermint
Pernod	Anise, licorice
Peter Heering	Black Danish cherry
Pistasha	Pistachio nut
Rock & Rye	Rocky candy, rye whiskey
Sambuca	Anise, licorice
Sloe Gin	Sloeberry (blackthorn)
Southern Comfort	Peach, honey, & Bourbon
Strega	Licorice, vanilla
Tia Maria	Sweet black coffee syrup
Triple Sec	Bitter orange
Vandermint	Chocolate mint
Yukon Jack	Peach

its or brandy. To this base, the flavoring materials are added. Figure 10.8 summarizes the flavoring of a wide variety of liqueurs.

Action Guidelines

✔ Design a wine list with recommendations on which wine goes well with each menu item.

✔ Develop a list of after-dinner drinks with a description of each one.

✔ Outline the elements of a talk that would accompany a wine tasting session.

✔ Outline the elements of a talk that would accompany a beer tasting session.

Chapter
11

RESPONSIBLE BUSINESS PRACTICES AND THE LAWS

A hospitality establishment serves its customers best when it serves them responsibly. Bar owners and employees should abide by the spirit and the letter of the liquor laws. It is estimated that 70 percent of the adult population drinks alcoholic beverages, to some degree. Servers of alcoholic beverages have a responsibility to help their customers have an enjoyable time without overindulging.

Know the Signs of Intoxication

Train your servers to always look for signs of intoxication. The challenge to a server is not to shut off a person, but to monitor their drinking in such a way that they have an enjoyable time without becoming intoxicated. The signs are the following:

- Lessening of inhibitions
- Exercising poor judgment
- Impairment of reaction time
- Loss of coordination

When people have a drink they tend to relax, their inhibitions lessen. Some become talkative, while others become quiet; but all are relaxing in their own way. If they drank at a pace of not more than one ounce of pure alcohol per hour (the liver's approximate limit for metabolizing alcohol), they could drink for quite a while without becoming intoxicated.

If they drink faster, their blood alcohol content rises, and they begin to demonstrate the first noticeable effects of intoxication; poor judgment, demonstrated by such signs as talking so loud as to irritate other customers, making outbursts of laughter or off-color remarks, becoming argumentative, and chug-a-lugging or ordering doubles.

Further drinking leads to a loss of reactions. This stage is reflected by such traits as slurring speech, fumbling with money or cigarettes, being unable to concentrate. The drinker's thoughts and motor skills are not synchronized.

The last stage, loss of coordination, is exhibited by stumbling and weaving, spilling drinks and dropping money, falling asleep, and a general inability to function normally.

It is important to keep drinkers out of the last two stages, because those are the stages where they can do harm to themselves and to others. Servers should be aware of the following conditions that influence the rate at which drinkers may become intoxicated and take precautions to prevent intoxication.

- Drinking too fast
- Repeatedly ordering strong drinks
- Taking medications while drinking
- Drinking on an empty stomach
- Drinking when depressed, stressed, or exhausted

In general, females have more fatty cells than males and tend to be smaller in body size. For those reasons, they tend to absorb alcohol into their bloodstream faster than males.

When servers are aware of a drinker's need to be slowed down, they can intervene by slowing down service, not asking for reorders right away, and offering snacks. When done tactfully, the customer may not even realize what is happening.

Responsible Business Practices

For some time, the issue of liability has been a major concern to operators of alcoholic beverage establishments. A great deal has been done by state agencies, the National Restaurant Association, the private training programs, and the major brewers and distillers of alcoholic beverages to educate the industry on the need for responsible business practices.

As a licensee and server of alcoholic beverages, you cannot eliminate your liability in issues involving alcohol, but you can certainly reduce your risk by establishing and adhering to responsible business practices, such as the following:

- Establishing sound policies and procedures and making sure all employees are acquainted with and practice them

- Letting your customers know what your policies are. Putting up posters and spelling out your policies on table tents, menus, and wine lists

- Keeping a list of all the things you do to abide by the law, such as conducting training sessions and checking IDs

- Keeping an incident log at your bar, into which bartenders and servers may enter a record of incidents where they had to shut off someone or refuse service to a person

- Checking the ID of anyone who does not appear to be at least 30 years old. This allows a comfortable margin of safety, as opposed to trying to determine if a person is 21 years old

- Setting a limit on the number of stronger drinks that may be served to a person or developing recipes for weaker versions of those drinks

- Sending your servers to training programs such as the TIPS program (Training for Intervention Procedures by Servers of Alcohol)

- Not having happy hours or similar programs that encourage people to consume excessive amounts of alcohol in short periods of time

- Making nonalcoholic drinks available

- Staffing adequately for peak periods, so that servers can check IDs without being rushed and monitor their customers properly

- Controlling the level of the lighting and music so that it does not encourage rapid drinking

- Offering free snacks to slow down consumption rates

- Offering free coffee to departing customers
- Calling taxi cabs, or arranging for safe transportation
- Conducting periodic, in-house, training sessions.

These kinds of activities establish you as a prudent, law-abiding businessperson that runs an ethical establishment with well-trained employees and high standards. Consequently, they can contribute positively to a defense, should one ever become necessary.

Liquor Laws

The Alcoholic Beverage Control agency of each state publishes its regulations, which are based on the statutes of that state. A copy of the regulations may be obtained by writing to or calling the agency. The laws and regulations vary from state to state, but two things are common throughout the 50 states and the District of Columbia.

1. You cannot legally serve a minor. For the purposes of drinking, a minor is defined as any person under age 21 years of age.
2. You cannot legally serve a person who is visibly intoxicated.

Checking IDs

It is imperative for a server of alcohol to check the ID of any person of questionable age. An *ID Checking Guide* may be obtained from the Drivers License Guide Company (telephone number 415-369-4849). The publication describes in detail, the specific features of drivers licenses of every state.

Following are some tips for checking the ID cards of persons of doubtful age:

- Hold the card in your hand. Do not check it in a wallet.
- Compare the picture on the ID with the face of the person.
- Check the date of birth on the card and ask the person what it is.
- Examine the card for signs of tampering. Feel the surface and look for discolorations, white-outs, or erasures.
- Check the thickness of the card to determine if the picture has been substituted.

Determining Who is Visibly Intoxicated

Few laws stipulate the standards for determining "visible intoxication." It is therefore important for servers to be trained to recognize the signs of intoxication and to always act prudently and within the law.

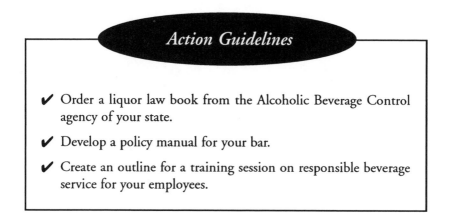

Action Guidelines

✔ Order a liquor law book from the Alcoholic Beverage Control agency of your state.

✔ Develop a policy manual for your bar.

✔ Create an outline for a training session on responsible beverage service for your employees.

Chapter
12

WHAT IF YOU SUCCEED —WHAT NEXT?

I f you focus on the 20 percent of the things that make 80 percent of the difference, and you do them well, there is a chance you will succeed in business. Many companies have started from humble beginnings and have grown to national proportions. Drive down any miracle mile and count the success stories.

If you do succeed, the inevitable questions will surface. What next? Stay as you are? Expand? Franchise? Or sell, and enjoy the profits? To decide what the right thing is for you to do, you will have to go back to square one and redefine your goals and objectives. You will have to evaluate the options and consider the sacrifices required by each. You will need to consider the implications of each possibility on your lifestyle and decide whether or not it is for you.

Should You Stay the Same?

Few businesses are able to remain the same for long periods of time. Even if a business is doing a good a job, changes are constantly occurring that affect it. Technology changes, consumer tastes change, new products come on to the market, economic conditions change, and new fads emerge. A business must respond to change if it is going to survive.

Some businesses have been able to incorporate changes, without sacrificing the concepts that initially made them successful. Managing change is said to be the biggest challenge most managers face throughout this decade.

Should You Expand?

This question has two facets: 1) should you expand? and 2) can you expand? If your sales have been steadily growing and trends point to continued growth, it would seem that expansion of some sort is advisable.

But, can you expand? Do you have the physical space to enlarge your operations. If you add on to your building, can you add on to your parking lot? How would the additional space integrate with your existing production system and flow of traffic? Can new equipment be placed where it is most needed?

If a business has the funds and foresight when it initially starts up, it should consider future expansion. Extra space can be left, in critical places, to allow for expansion of a production line. Plumbing, heating, ventilation, and air conditioning systems can be planned with an eye to the future.

It is unfortunate when a business has to move because it outgrows its present location and cannot expand there. One never knows if the dynamics that worked so well in the original setting will happen again in the new facility. Customers sometimes resent change and will try a competitor before following a business.

Should You Franchise?

This is an option that many businesses flirt with, but very few consider it seriously, because it requires a great deal of legal and financial expertise, as well as a substantial amount of capital. One must be realistic in assessing whether the business, or concept is franchisable. Does it have universal appeal? Is it unique enough to fill an existing market niche?

Many businesses open up additional company-owned locations, as an alternative to franchising and all of its complexities.

Should You Sell the Business?

There are people that are very successful at starting and growing businesses, then selling them for substantial gains on their investment. Those people enjoy the challenge of creating a successful business, but care very little about running it once the fun is over.

If your business does succeed, you will be in an enviable position to evaluate, without any financial pressures, whether you want to continue in it. You must ask yourself if you are happy with your lifestyle, and if you are getting the satisfaction you anticipated out of the business? If the answers to those questions are "no," you should probably sell the business, and enjoy the profit from the sale. On the other hand, if the answers are "yes," and you remain in the business and continue to do a good job, you should make a very good living and be happy in your work.

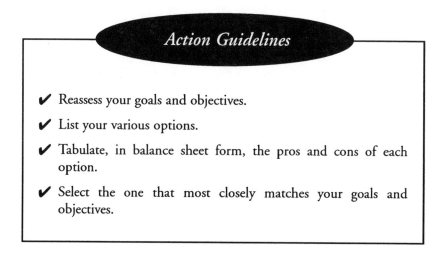

Action Guidelines

✔ Reassess your goals and objectives.

✔ List your various options.

✔ Tabulate, in balance sheet form, the pros and cons of each option.

✔ Select the one that most closely matches your goals and objectives.

Appendix
A

SAMPLE LOAN APPLICATION AND BUSINESS PLAN

Developing a business plan is a critical part of the process of starting a business. It can be used to convince investors or lenders of the soundness of a proposed business. In addition, it can be used as a business guide during the early stages of a new enterprise. Chapter 4 describes the elements of a business plan in detail. Following is an illustration of how a business plan for an upscale, urban bar and grill might appear.

Sample Loan Application

Loan Application

Applicants
John Q. Public and James Public (father and son, partners)
123 Central Street
Yourtown, MA 01909
Tel. (617) 555-7891

Business
The Ticker Tape Bar & Grill
One Financial Plaza
Capital City, MA 02202

Type of Business
Tavern: Serving cafe food and all alcoholic beverages

Size of Business
Annual sales volume of $760,716

Type of Ownership
General Partnership - 5/6 share John Q. Public
1/6 share James Public

Funds to be Contributed by Applicants
John Q. Public will invest $125,000 cash in the business and James Public
will invest $25,000. The equity in John Q. Public's fully owned home,
which is appraised at $250,000 (current market value) will be pledged as
collateral to secure the loan.

Other Contributions by Applicants
John Q. Public has 25 years experience in the bar business, 15 years as a
bartender and 10 years as a manager. James Public has a college degree in
food and beverage management.

Loan Request and Intended Use of Funds

Amount Requested
$150,000

Term of Loan
15 years, with no prepayment penalty. First payment due three months after transaction date of loan.

Interest Rate
Bank's current lending rate—12% fixed rate

Debt to Equity Ratio
1 to 1 ($150,000 to $150,000)

Collateral
Mortgage on the wholly owned home of John Q. Public. Current market value appraised at $250,000.

Other Protections
Borrowers will carry insurance against business interruption and loss due to hazards, naming the lender as a beneficiary in the event of interruption of business.

Intended Use of Funds
The partners will use the funds, in conjunction with their own invest-ment, to acquire a license, obtain a lease, make improvements to the leased premises, purchase furniture, fixtures, equipment and inventories necessary to open **The Ticker Tape Bar & Grill** and conduct a Grand Opening.

Following is a Sample Business Plan for a Bar and Grill

BUSINESS PLAN

The Ticker Tape Bar & Grill
One Financial Plaza
Capital City, MA 02202

November 1, 1994

John Q. Public and James Public (Partners)
123 Central Street
Yourtown, MA 01909

Telephone:
(617) 555-7891

Copy No. 1

Table of Contents

Statement of Purpose

John Q. and James Public, copartners, seek a loan of $150,000, which together with their $150,000 personal investment, will be used to acquire a license; obtain a lease at One Financial Plaza, Capital City, Massachusetts, make improvements to the leased premises, purchase furniture, fixtures, equipment and inventories, provide working capital for two months, and cover such other pre-opening expenses that are necessary to open **The Ticker Tape Bar & Grill.** It is expected that the business will produce a profit in the first year, and increased profits are expected in subsequent years, assuring a timely payback of the loan.

Part One: The Business

Background. Recognizing that the only food or beverage service at One Financial Plaza is a fast food establishment that has a very limited menu and serves only soft drinks, the principals sensed that the needs of most of the professional occupants of the building were not being met. A survey was conducted throughout the building, which houses 4,000 employees, and it was determined that a bar and grill with light food and an upscale ambiance would be most welcome. Coupled with the fact that the new Metropolitan Civic Center will bring thousands of people into the area for events and conventions, it appeared a bar and grill would be very successful at this location.

The Ticker Tape Bar & Grill will occupy 2,400 square feet of space, and will have a capacity of 100 seats. Its hours of service will be 11 A.M. to 12 P.M., seven days a week, however, food service will cease at 10 P.M.

Entertainment will consist of two television sets located at the bar and piped-in background music in the daytime. A piano player will play cocktail music from 6 P.M. to 10 P.M., on Thursdays through Saturday.

Mission Statement. The Ticker Tape Bar & Grill seeks to serve high quality food and beverages in a friendly atmosphere, while observing the highest standards of responsible beverage service.

The Concept. The Ticker Tape Bar & Grill will be an upscale bar, serving liquor, beer, wine, and café food in a unique setting. Its decor will be that of a 1920s stock brokerage office, with ticker tape machines and a large blackboard showing 1929 stock prices. Dark mahogany paneled walls will feature poster size pictures of famous millionaires and old front pages of the *Wall Street Journal.* Lighting will be from old-fashioned office chandeliers, and menu covers will be replicas of stock and bond certificates. Tables will have round, marble tops and sturdy captain's chairs.

Location. The business will be located on the ground floor of One Financial Plaza, a professional building with approximately 4,000 employees, occupied primarily by investment, law, and accounting firms. A favorable eight-year lease, with an option to renew, has been arranged at $19.31 per square foot.

The location is one block away from the soon to be completed Metropolitan Civic Center. The Civic Center's conventions and events are expected to generate up to 1 million visitors to the area, and the Ticker Tape Bar & Grill will be its closest upscale bar.

Access to the Ticker Tape Bar & Grill is available from the lobby of the building, from the street, and from the parking garage. There is a 1,000 car subterranean parking garage directly beneath One Financial Plaza, and a subway station entrance across the street.

Industry Trends. Studies by several state and local governmental agencies indicate the emerging pattern of economic growth in the greater Capital City area is expected to continue over the next decade, as a result of the emergence of several high tech industries. The highly attractive pool of scientists, engineers, and medical professionals, continues to make this an ideal location for such industries.

The expected growth, coupled with the major infusion of tourists attracted by events at the new Civic Center, will substantially benefit the retail and hospitality sectors of the local economy. The Ticker Tape Bar & Grill is located in a prime position, at One Financial Plaza, to benefit from the growth.

The Management. John Q. Public will manage The Ticker Tape Bar & Grill. He will also function as daytime head bartender. James Public will be head chef, and Mary L. Public, James's sister, head waitress.

John Q. Public has 15 years experience as a bartender and head bartender for a major Capital City hotel and 10 years experience as the general manager of a prominent café.

James Public has an associate degree in hospitality management with a major in culinary arts. He has two years experience as a bartender, eight years experience as second cook and night chef for a major hotel.

Mary Public has four years of waitressing experience at an upscale bar and grill in San Francisco.

Objectives and Financial Expectations. The immediate goal of the management is to generate a cash flow sufficient to meet all obligations of the business and generate an after tax net profit of 10% of total sales, accomplished through creative merchandising, intensive advertising and the utilization of cost controls.

(2)

The long-term goal of the management is to become one of Capital City's premier bars—an establishment noted for its unique ambiance, its excellent bar service, and its superb food—and to attain an annual return on investment in excess of 20% for its owners.

Product and Service. The Ticker Tape Bar & Grill will be unique to the Capital City area. Its style of service and method of food presentation will be similar to that of the famous San Francisco grills, and its stock market decor will be refreshingly appealing to the targeted clientele.

The clear message at the Ticker Tape Bar & Grill is "this is an excellent bar that also serves excellent food," not a restaurant that also serves drinks.

The menu will feature steaks, chops, ribs, beef kabobs, and other grill items, as well as upscale sandwich plates such as Reubens and Monte Carlos, taco salads, burritos, and finger foods. No other restaurant in the marketing area offers a similar grill menu.

Pricing and Profitability. The Ticker Tape Bar & Grill's bar will operate with a bar cost percentage of 20%. It's grill will operate with food cost percentage of 30%.

With the expected percentage breakdown of total sales to be 52% food sales and 48% beverage sales, the combined cost of sales will be 25.2%, producing a gross profit of 74.8% on total sales.

Prices will be competitive with other upscale bars. However, it is the strategy of The Ticker Tape Bar & Grill to give a perception of higher value than its competitors, through its food and drink presentation methods.

Product Life Cycle. Due to the uniqueness of the stock market concept, The Ticker Tape Bar & Grill has an indeterminate life cycle. At the end of the business's fifth year, however, the management will conduct a self-study to determine if the concept and the menu need to be rejuvenated.

It is expected that due to normal wear and tear, the facility will need a complete refurbishing and replacement of some equipment in seven years.

Market Analysis. The growth that is expected to result from the construction of the new Civic Center has been well determined by public and private research projects. Four thousand employees work at One Financial

(3)

Plaza. An estimated 3,000 business people and retail shoppers visit the complex every business day. Seventy percent of the city's most famous specialty shops are located within three blocks of One Financial Plaza. Many people visit the complex to see its highly regarded architecture. Its subterranean parking garage accommodates more than 1,000 tourists and commuters each day because of its central location. Three major universities are located within a 10-minute subway ride.

Civic Center visitors who exit from the subway station and the parking garage will be within eye view of The Ticker Tape Bar & Grill, which has an exterior entrance as well as a lobby entrance.

Two surveys of the occupants of the building indicate a desire for an upscale bar and grill to which they may bring business guests for food and beverages. The Ticker Tape Bar & Grill fills a need, and has no competition offering the same concept within its marketing area.

Competition. There are three bars, two fast food restaurants and a full-service restaurant within three blocks of the Ticker Tape Bar & Grill. One of the fast food restaurants is located at One Financial Plaza, but has a very limited menu and no alcoholic beverage service. None of these are as easily accessible to the target clientele as the Ticker Tape Bar & Grill and none offer a similar concept.

The two fast food establishments cater mainly to youths and lower paid retail and service workers. One of the bars is a sports bar that serves only pizza and submarine sandwiches. The other two are taverns that do not offer food menus. The full-service restaurant is a well-established, moderately priced Italian-American restaurant, with a loyal clientele. It is located on a dead-end side street and is the furthest, of the five potential competitors, from One Financial Plaza and the Metropolitan Civic Center.

Studies determined that none of the competitors presented substantial competition because of their different concepts and menu offerings.

Customers. The Ticker Tape Bar & Grill will have two types of customers. One is the professional and administrative workers of One Financial Plaza and nearby office buildings. The other is visitors, shoppers, tourists, and Civic Center attendees.

The first type will typically have the following characteristics: Males or females, over 25, with some degree of post high school education or train-

(4)

year. Most of them will commute from suburban communities and will park in the underground garage. At the present time, there is no food and beverage establishment in close proximity serving the needs of this segment of the market.

The second type of customers are most likely to be discriminating diners, who prefer an upscale bar or restaurant that offers good drinks and lighter foods. They like to converse with friends and appreciate quiet background music and a unique atmosphere. They will probably be on a shopping trip or attending an event at the Civic Center. Their demographics will match closely with those of the first type of customers.

Marketing Strategy. In the daytime, the Ticker Tape Bar & Grill will be positioned as a trendy place to bring your business and personal friends for good light food, superb drinks, and quiet conversation—a place where you can see and be seen by important people in the business and social community. A place where introductions and networking are common.

In the evening, it will be positioned as a unique piano bar that serves excellent light food and delicious drinks. It will appeal to busy people who seek a relaxing atmosphere for socializing, as well as to tourists and patrons of Civic Center events. Contacts will be made with taxi companies, tour group leaders, and other persons who make recommendations or plan activities for tourists.

All advertisements and commercials will position the Ticker Tape Bar & Grill as an alternative to loud and smoky bars. The Frankel and Franco Advertising Agency, with more then 12 years of successful experience with hospitality accounts in the Capital City area, will handle all advertising placements and public relations releases.

Support will be given to a number of charitable and community causes, and the owners of the business will be active members of the Chamber of Commerce, Rotary, and Kiwanis clubs.

Personnel. The staff will include 11 full-time employees and 10 part-time employees, who in total will work an average of 629 hours per week and generate an average weekly payroll of $3,862.

The estimated annual payroll of $200,829.20 is 29.9% of total sales. Table 1 shows the employee work schedule for the Ticker Tape Bar & Grill. Arrangements have been made for additional, temporary staffing on nights when special events are scheduled at the Civic Center.

Employee Work Schedule

	Mon.	Tue.	Wed.	Thur.	Fri.	Sat.	Sun.	Total Hours	Hourly Rate	Weekly Pay
Bar Personnel										
Day Head Bartender	10/6	10/6	10/6	10/6	10/6			40	8.00	320.00
Night Head Bartender					5/1	5/1	5/1	40	7.00	280.00
Bartender, Part-time	11/2	11/2	11/2	11/2	11/2			15	6.00	90.00
Bartender, Part-time	5/1	5/1				6/1	6/10	24	5.50	132.00
Bartender, Part-time						10/6	10/6	32	5.50	176.00
Bartender, Part-time	6/9	6/9	6/9	6/9	6/1	11/2	11/2	12	5.50	66.00
Wait Staff										
Day Head Waitperson	10/4		10/4	10/4	10/4	10/4	10/4	36	3.40	122.40
Night Head Waitperson		4/10	4/10	4/10	4/10	4/10	4/10	36	3.25	117.00
Waitperson, Part-time	11/2	10/4	11/2	11/2	11/2	11/2		18	2.95	53.10
Waitperson, Part-time	4/10	11/2	11/2	11/2	11/2	11/2		18	2.95	53.10
Waitperson, Part-time	11/2				11/2			12	2.95	35.40
Waitperson, Part-time			5/10	5/10	5/10	5/10	11/2	24	2.95	70.80
Waitperson, Part-time		5/9	5/9	5/9	5/9	5/10	5/9	21	2.95	61.95
Waitperson, Part-time	5/9		5/9	5/9			5/9	13	2.95	38.35
Kitchen Personnel										
Head Chef	5/10	9/5	9/5	9/5	9/5	9/5	9/5	48	12.00	576.00
Night Chef	9/5	5/10	5/10	5/10	5/10	5/10	5/10	30	10.00	300.00
Rounds Person	5/10	5/10		5/10	11/7	11/7	5/11	40	8.00	320.00
Cooks Helper	5/10	5/10	5/10		5/10	5/10	5/10	54	6.00	324.00
Salad Maker	11/7	11/7	11/7	11/7			11/7	54	6.00	324.00
Dishwasher & Porter	11/7	11/7	11/7	11/7	11/7	11/7	11/7	32	6.00	192.00
Dishwasher	5/10	5/10	5/10	5/10	5/11		5/11	30	7.00	210.00

Total Weekly Payroll	$ 3,862.10
Times 52 Weeks	x 52
Est. Annual Payroll	$200,829.20

nights when special events are scheduled at the Civic Center.

Risk. Risk management will be practiced from the opening day. All service employees will be required to attend an accredited Responsible Alcohol Service Course. Food service workers will all be required to take the National Food Service Sanitation Course. Both courses will entitle the bar to substantial discounts on insurance premiums.

The Ticker Tape Bar & Grill will carry the following insurance policies:

• Liquor Liability Insurance and Third Party Liability
• Workers' Compensation Insurance
• General Liability Insurance
• Business Interruption Insurance
• Product Liability Insurance
• Fire Insurance
• Key Person Life Insurance on Partners
• Personal Injury Liability Insurance

In addition to insuring against risk, ongoing training programs will be conducted to ensure a high degree of professionalism among employees.

Loan Request and Intended Use of Funds

Amount Requested
$150,000

Term of Loan
Fifteen years, with no prepayment penalty. First payment due three months after transaction date of loan.

Interest Rate
Bank's current lending rate—12% fixed rate.

Debt to Equity Ratio
1 to 1 ($150,000 to $150,000)

Collateral
Mortgage on the wholly owned home of John Q. Public. Current market value appraised at $250,000.

Other Protections
Borrowers will carry insurance against business interruption and loss due to hazards, naming the lender as a beneficiary in the event of interruption of business.

Intended Use of Funds
The partners will use the borrowed funds, in conjunction with their own investment, to acquire a license, secure a lease, make improvements to the leased premises, purchase furniture, fixtures, equipment and inventories necessary to open **The Ticker Tape Bar & Grill** and conduct a Grand Opening.

Summary of Part One

John Q. Public and his son, James Public seek a collateralized loan of $150,000, which in conjunction with their combined personal investment of $150,000 will be used to open an upscale bar and grill at One Financial Plaza, Capital City. Extensive market analysis shows a need for such a facility, and a sufficient target population to sustain it. The new Metropolitan Civic Center, which will be located one block away, is expected to bring an additional 1 million people into the area every year.

The establishment, to be known as The Ticker Tape Bar and Grill, will have a capacity of 100 seats and will offer high quality food and beverage service in a unique atmosphere. Its decor will resemble a 1920s stock brokerage office. Surveys show it will be a welcomed alternative to loud and smoky competitors. There is no other direct competition in its dominant marketing area.

It is expected that through effective sales promotion and the use of cost controls, the business will be profitable from the first year, and will be able to pay back the loan and the partners' investment in six years.

The target market will be administrative and professional employees of One Financial and nearby office buildings, who go out to lunch every day and often entertain business guests.

Part Two: Financial Projections

Start-Up Requirements

Cash (working capital)	$15,000
Leasehold Improvements	64,480
License	35,000
Beginning Inventories	
(Food, Beverages and Supplies)	20,000
Furniture, Fixtures, and Equipment	129,694
Opening Expenses	
Liquor liability insurance, other insurances, licenses, permits, clean up, advertising and promotion, deposits, employee training, pre-opening parties, and grand opening	35,826
Total Start-Up Investment Required	**$300,000**

Estimated Annual Sales

No. of Customers Expected Per Week
(sum of daily estimates)

	Total
Lunch	573
Dinner	417
Bar Only	205
Total Customers per Week	*1,195*

Average Menu Prices

Sandwiches and Salads	$4.95
Entrees	8.95
Desserts	2.75
Drinks	2.75

Estimated Average Guest Check Per Person

Lunch	Sandwich or Salad plus Drink	$ 6.35
Dinner	Entree, Salad, Dessert,	
	plus Drinks	22.79
Bar Only	Average 2 Drinks	5.50

Estimated Weekly Sales

573 customers	x	$ 6.35	=	$3,638
417 customers	x	22.79	=	9,504
205 customers	x	5.50	=	1,127

Total Weekly Sales $14,269

Estimated Annual Sales

52 weeks	x	$14,629	=	$760,716

(11)

List of Furniture, Fixtures, and Equipment

Qty.	Item	Cost
1	Ice maker, air-cooled, 600-pound capacity	$3,500
1	Remote, 6-keg capacity, beer refrigerator	2,700
2	Cocktail stations, 30"	2,100
2	Three compartment bar sinks with speed racks and double drain boards	1,500
1	Direct draw, 3-keg beer box with taps	2,300
2	Post mix soda dispensing systems, with carbonator and 50' lines	2,100
1	Three door bar refrigerator	2,700
1	Glass froster, 3', 120-mug capacity	1,400
1	Beer bottle cooler, 4'	1,200
1	20' Front bar with top and foot rail	4,320
1	14' Back bar with cabinets and shelves	2,338
10	Bar stools, upholstered	3,000
7	Booths, 4'	4,313
11	Lounge tables, with bases, seat 4	2,189
9	Cocktail tables, with bases, seat 2	1,575
62	Chairs	9,300
2	Television sets	4,500
	Glassware	1,100
	Small bar wares and supplies	1,800
1	Safe, fireproof	3,000
1	Wine cellar, redwood, refrigerated	5,575
1	Cash register	2,250
1	Desk, mahogany and swivel chair	625
1	Desk, steel and secretary's chair	450
1	Planter, divider, 3' high	515
1	Dishwasher, automatic	11,300
1	Freezer, reach in, stainless, with racks	3,725
2	Fryers, twin basket	7,450
1	Griddle, 3'	3,500
1	Toaster, automatic, conveyor type	1,725
2	Stainless steel prep tables	800
1	Food mixer, 20 quart	3,175

(12)

1 Restaurant range	2,550
1 Convection oven	5,450
1 Garbage disposer	294
2 Refrigerators, 40 cu. ft., stainless	4,475
1 Fire protection hood and exhaust system	10,000
1 Broiler	2,800
1 Coffee urn	2,100

Total Cost of Furniture, Fixtures, and Equipment	*$129,694*

Leasehold Improvements

Heating, ventilation, and air conditioning	$17,280
Electrical	15,920
Plumbing	12,000
Carpeting, floor tile, and other related equipment	19,280

Total Leasehold Improvements	*$64,480*

Sources and Uses of Funds

Uses of Funds	Source of Funds		
Start-Up Expenses	Partners' Equity	Loan	Total
Furniture, Fixtures, and Equipment	$47,347	$82,347	$129,694
Leasehold Improvements	32,240	32,240	64,480
License	35,000	0	35,000
Food, Beverage, and Supplies Inventories	10,000	10,000	20,000
Opening Expenses	17,913	17,913	35,826
Liquor Liability Insurance, other insurances, licenses, permits, advertising, lease deposit, clean up, employee training, pre-opening parties and Grand Opening			
Working Capital	7,500	7,500	15,000
Total Funds	**$150,000**	**$150,000**	**$300,000**

Income Statement
The Ticker Tape Bar & Grill
for the period of January 1 through December 31, 199—

			Percentages
Sales			
Food Sales	$395,572		52.0
Beverage Sales	$365,144		48.0
Total Sales		$760,716	100.0
Cost of Sales			
Food Cost	$118,672		30.0
Beverage Cost	73,028		20.0
Total Cost of Sales		$191,700	25.2
Gross Profit from Operations		$569,016	74.8
Other Income		2,282	0.3
Total Income		$571,298	75.1
Controllable Expenses			
Payroll	$200,829		26.4
Employee Benefits	30,429		4.0
Direct Operating Expenses	43,361		5.7
Advertising and Promotion	22,061		2.9
Music and Entertainment	15,214		2.0
Utilities	24,343		3.2
Administrative and General Expenses	30,429		4.0
Repairs and Maintenance	15,214		2.0
Total Controlable Expenses		$381,880	50.2
Profit Before Occupancy Costs		$189,418	24.9
Occupancy Costs			
Rent	$38,796		5.1
Property Taxes	4,564		0.6
Other Taxes	1,521		0.2
Property Insurance	7,607		1.0
Total Occupancy Costs		$52,488	
Profit Before Interest and Depreciation		$136,930	18.0
Interest		3,804	0.5
Depreciation		15,216	2.0
Net Profit Before Tax		117,910	15.5

(15)

PROJECTED INCOME STATEMENT
The Ticker Tape Bar and Grill
For the period of January 1 through December 31, 199—

	JAN	FEB	MAR	APR	MAY	JUN	JUL	AUG	SEP	OCT	NOV	DEC	TOTAL
Sales													
Food	24,960	26,000	27,560	28,600	29,120	30,680	32,760	35,360	36,400	38,480	40,040	45,612	395,572
Beverage	23,040	24,000	25,440	26,400	26,880	28,320	30,240	32,640	33,600	35,520	36,960	42,104	365,144
Total Sales	48,000	50,000	53,000	55,000	56,000	59,000	63,000	68,000	70,000	74,000	77,000	87,716	760,716
Cost of Sales													
Food	7,488	7,800	8,268	8,580	8,736	9,204	9,828	10,608	10,920	11,544	12,012	13,684	118,672
Beverage	4,608	4,800	5,088	5,280	5,376	5,664	6,048	6,528	6,720	7,104	7,392	8,421	73,029
Total Cost of Sales	12,096	12,600	13,356	13,860	14,112	14,868	15,876	17,136	17,640	18,648	19,404	22,104	191,700
Gross Profit from Operations	35,904	37,400	39,644	41,140	41,888	44,132	47,124	50,864	52,360	55,352	57,596	65,612	569,016
Other Income	144	150	159	165	168	177	189	204	210	222	231	263	2,282
Total Income	36,048	37,550	39,803	41,305	42,056	44,309	47,313	51,068	52,570	55,574	57,827	65,875	571,298
Controllable Expenses													
Payroll	12,480	13,000	13,780	14,300	14,560	15,340	16,380	17,680	18,200	19,240	21,520	24,349	200,829
Employee Benefits	1,920	2,000	2,120	2,200	2,240	2,360	2,520	2,720	2,800	2,960	3,080	3,509	30,429
Direct Operating	2,736	2,850	3,021	3,135	3,192	3,363	3,591	3,876	3,990	4,218	4,389	5,000	43,361
Advertising and Promotion	1,392	1,450	1,537	1,595	1,624	1,711	1,827	1,972	2,030	2,146	2,233	2,544	22,061
Music and Entertainment	960	1,000	1,060	1,100	1,120	1,180	1,260	1,360	1,400	1,480	1,540	1,754	15,214
Utilities	1,536	1,600	1,696	1,760	1,792	1,888	2,016	2,176	2,240	2,368	2,464	2,807	24,343
Administrative and Gen.	1,920	2,000	2,120	2,200	2,240	2,360	2,520	2,720	2,800	2,960	3,080	3,509	30,429
Repairs and Maintenance	960	1,000	1,060	1,100	1,120	1,180	1,260	1,360	1,400	1,480	1,540	1,754	15,214
Total Controllable Expenses	23,904	24,900	26,394	27,390	27,848	29,382	31,374	33,864	34,860	36,852	39,846	45,226	381,880
Profit Before Occupancy Costs	12,144	12,650	13,409	13,915	14,168	14,927	15,939	17,204	17,710	18,722	17,981	20,649	189,418
Occupancy Costs													
Rent	3,233	3,233	3,233	3,233	3,233	3,233	3,233	3,233	3,233	3,233	3,233	3,233	38,796
Property Taxes	380	380	380	380	380	380	380	380	380	380	380	384	4,564
Other Taxes	127	127	127	127	127	127	127	127	127	127	127	124	1,521
Property Insurance	634	634	634	634	634	634	634	634	634	634	634	634	7,607
Total Occupancy Costs	4,374	4,374	4,374	4,374	4,374	4,374	4,374	4,374	4,374	4,374	4,374	4,373	52,488
Profit Before Int. and Depr.	7,770	8,276	9,035	9,541	9,794	10,553	11,565	12,830	13,336	14,348	13,607	16,275	136,930
Interest	317	317	317	317	317	317	317	317	317	317	317	317	3,804
Depreciation	1,268	1,268	1,268	1,268	1,268	1,268	1,268	1,268	1,268	1,268	1,268	1,268	15,216
NET PROFIT BEFORE TAXES	6,185	6,691	7,450	7,956	8,209	8,968	9,980	11,245	11,751	12,763	12,022	14,690	117,910

CASH FLOW STATEMENT—BY MONTH
The Ticker Tape Bar and Grill
For the period of January 1 through December 31, 199—

SOURCES OF CASH	PRE-OPENING	JAN	FEB	MAR	APR	MAY	JUN	JUL	AUG	SEPT	OCT	NOV	DEC	TOTAL
Partner's Equity	150,000													150,000
Loan	150,000													150,000
Net Profit	0	6,185	6,691	7,450	7,956	8,209	8,968	9,980	11,245	11,751	12,763	13,522	16,233	120,953
Depreciation	0	1,268	1,268	1,268	1,268	1,268	1,268	1,268	1,268	1,268	1,268	1,268	1,268	15,216
TOTAL	300,000	7,453	7,959	8,718	9,224	9,477	10,236	11,248	12,513	13,019	14,031	14,790	17,501	436,169
DISBURSEMENTS														
Liquor License	35,000													35,000
Leasehold Improv.	64,480													64,480
Furn./Fix./Equip.	129,694													129,964
Beg. Inventories	20,000													20,000
Opening Costs	35,826													35,826
Mo. Loan Paymts.	0	0	1,809	1,809	1,809	1,809	1,809	1,809	1,809	1,809	1,809	1,809	1,809	19,899
Income Taxes	0	2,474	2,676	2,980	3,182	3,284	3,587	3,992	4,498	4,700	5,105	4,809	5,876	47,163
TOTAL	285,000	2,474	4,485	4,789	4,991	5,093	5,396	5,801	6,307	6,509	6,914	6,618	7,685	352,332
MO. CASH FLOW	15,000	4,979	3,474	3,929	4,233	4,384	4,840	5,447	6,206	6,510	7,117	8,172	9,816	84,107
CUM. CASH FLOW	15,000	19,979	23,453	27,832	31,615	35,989	40,839	46,286	52,492	59,002	66,119	74,291	84,107	84,107

Daily Break-Even Analysis

Monthly Fixed Costs

Rent	$ 3,233
Salaries	8,548
Utilities	2,029
Insurance	1,055
Taxes	605
Depreciation	1,268
Total Monthly Fixed Costs	$16,738

Daily Fixed Costs (Total Monthly Fixed Cost ÷ 30 days)	**$ 558**

Daily Variable Costs

Cost of Food (one day's supply)	$ 330
Cost of Liquor (one day's supply)	203
Cost of Additional Staff Essential to Sales	357
Total Daily Variable Costs	**$ 890**
Daily Sales Volume Required To Break-Even	**$ 1,448**

(18)

Conclusion and Summary

This request is for a secured loan in the amount of $150,000, which together with an investment of $150,000 by John Q. and James Public (partners), will be used to start The Ticker Tape Bar & Grill. Specifically, the funds will be used to acquire a license; obtain a lease for premises at One Financial Plaza; purchase furniture, fixtures, equipment ,and inventories; hire and train a staff; and for pre-opening expenses and working capital.

All financial projections have been made conservatively, with a 10% safety factor used to overstate costs and to understate revenues. It is expected that The Ticker Tape Bar & Grill will operate profitably in its first year of operation and be able to meet all of its obligations in a timely manner.

The opening of the nearby Metropolitan Civic Center will attract over one million tourists, sports fans, and conventioneers to the dominant marketing area of The Ticker Tape Bar & Grill each year. This expansion of the market, coupled with aggressive marketing and strict cost controls, should enable profits to grow for the foreseeable future.

(19)

Part Three: Supporting Documents

Résumé

John Q. Public
123 Central Street
Yourtown, MA 01909
Tel. (617) 555-7891

Education
Eastern Regional High School, Middle Field, MA.

Employment
The Bradshaw Hotel, Capital City, MA, 1969-1984
Position: Bartender and Head Bartender

Charles River Café, 1984-1994
Position: General Manager

Personal Credit References
Seacoast Savings Bank
House mortgage, paid up in 1992

First State Bank, Boston, MA
Automobile Loan, 36 months, paid up, 1993

Personal: Born: April 15, 1947, Camtree, MA
Married, one son, James and one daughter, Mary

References

Amos Lard, President	Jeremy Vender, Sales Manager
Third Institute of Savings	Formidable Insurance Company
503 Flint Street	1520 Granite Road
Capital City, MA 02200	Capital City, MA 02200

(20)

Résumé

James Public
123 Central Street
Yourtown, MA 02209
Tel. (617) 456-7891

Education
Back Bay Community College, Capital City, MA
A.S. Hospitality Management, 1984

Employment
Bradshaw Hotel, Boston, MA, 1984-1994
Positions: Bartender, 2nd Cook, Night Chef

Personal Credit References
Seacoast Savings Bank
Automobile loan, paid up in 1992

Downtown National Bank, Capital City, MA
Boat Loan, 24 months, paid up, 1994

References
Angela Marsden, Executive Director
Bayside Chamber of Commerce
590 Front Street
Capital City, MA 02202

Marcia Winder, Advertising Manager
Broader & Broader Advertising Agency
117 Maynard Avenue
Capital City, MA 02203

Personal Balance Sheet
John Q. Public
as of November 1, 1994

Assets

Cash in Bank—Savings	$ 5,000
Checking	3,000
Marketable Securities	65,000
Life Insurance	80,000
Real Estate (Current Market Value)	250,000
Automobile	18,000
Other Personal Assets	16,000
Total Assets	**$437,000**

Liabilities

Accounts Payable	$ 9,500
Automobile Installment Loan	14,000
Total Liabilities	**$ 23,500**

NET WORTH	**$413,500**
TOTAL LIABILITIES PLUS NET WORTH	**$437,000**

(22)

Personal Balance Sheet
James Public
as of November 1, 1994

Assets

Cash in Bank—Savings	$ 13,300
Checking	2,500
Marketable Securities	28,000
Automobile	10,000
Other Personal Assets	6,000
Total Assets	**$ 59,800**

Liabilities

Accounts Payable	$ 2,100
Automobile Installment Loan	7,200
Total Liabilities	**$ 9,300**

NET WORTH	**$ 50,500**
TOTAL LIABILITIES PLUS NET WORTH	**$ 59,800**

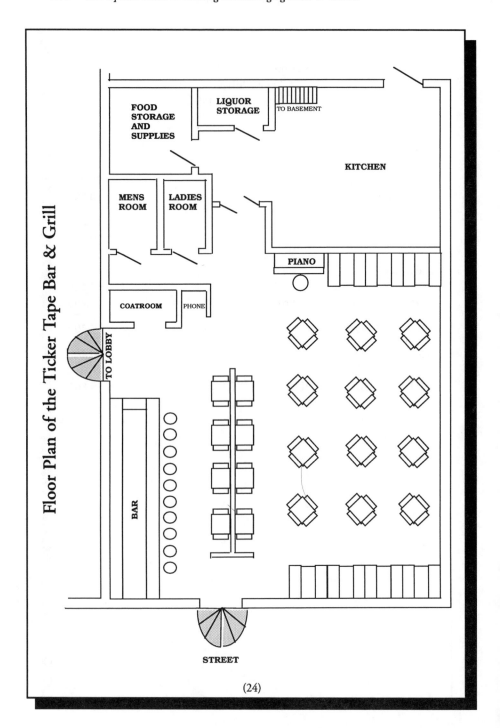

Floor Plan of the Ticker Tape Bar & Grill

(24)

BARTENDER ROUTINES

Typical Opening Routine for a Daytime Bartender

1. Oversees cleanup by porters (unless the cleanup is done at night after closing).

2. Cash register is cleared (by someone other than the bartender). Counts bank in register.

3. Checks and restocks beer box and draught beer supply.

4. Counts number of empty bottles and marks on inventory sheets (to be used for drawing full bottles out of storeroom).

5. Checks and restocks supply of napkins, soda, sugar, stirrers and straws, and lemon mix.

6. Draws liquor from storeroom (wine cellar) and brings supplies out from kitchen.

7. Opens faucets to run out stale water. (Run for several minutes).

8. Runs two gallons of hot water through draught beer drain grill (to prevent clogging).

9. Makes pre-mix lemon juice.

10. Wipes down stainless steel and bar surfaces.

11. Stocks ice bins with crushed and cube ice.

12. Cuts up fruit. Puts fruit in dispensing containers for bartenders and wait staff.

13. Inspects bar and lounge for overall cleanliness and appearance.
14. OPENS UP FOR BUSINESS.

Typical Routine for a Night Bartender

1. Counts bank. Makes out change request and obtains necessary change for banks.
2. Makes sure any bar glasses washed in the kitchen have been returned to the bar.
3. Double checks all supplies before day bartender leaves.
4. Make sure cash register is cleared (by other than a bartender) and night bartender inserts his or her bank.
5. STARTS WORK. MIXES DRINKS. SERVES CUSTOMERS. HANDLES CASH.
6. At end of shift, stacks all empties in cartons.
7. Washes and puts away all dirty glasses.
8. General cleanup. Stainless steel, sinks, bar, etc.
9. Takes apart glass washer and allows brushes to dry overnight.
10. Locks up bar.

Weekly Bar Routines

1. Clean out beer box thoroughly.
2. Clean out wine and liquor cabinets.
3. Flush out beer lines (essential for serving high-quality draught beer.)

Bartender's Closing Duties

1. Locks all doors from inside.
2. Washes glasses and puts them away.
3. Checks restrooms and other areas for slow patrons.
4. Drains sinks (one sink at a time).
5. Refrigerates fruit and perishable items.

6. Secures cash in authorized location.

7. Checks entire premises for burning cigarettes.

8. Adjusts thermostats for night temperature.

9. Fill beer storage boxes (this may also be done in the morning).

10. Wipes bar top thoroughly with damp rag and soda.

11. Turns off outside lights (illuminated signs).

12. Sets and tests burglar alarm set and tested.

13. Turns inside lights off, except for safety light.

14. Makes final inspection before leaving.

Do not allow a customer to come back inside after all customers are out and the door is locked from the inside regardless of the problem. You may prevent a holdup.

The Secret to Bigger Tips

The secret to bigger tips is better service. Here are four suggestions on how you can give your customers better services.

1. Know the brands you carry. It is impractical for bars to stock every conceivable brand of liquor on the market. If you know your brands, you can suggest something comparable when a customer orders something you do not carry.

2. Pay attention to customers' special requests. For example, if a customer asks for a "very, very dry martini," don't give him a heavy handed dash of dry vermouth. Try to give the appearance of measuring the tiny amount with care and precision, and do it in view of the customer if possible. This is part of the showmanship and presentation that makes bartenders look good.

3. Try to do something extra for every customer at the bar. Wipe the bar, empty an ash tray, change a napkin, offer matches, whatever is appropriate and applicable. This is almost a mental attitude— look for ways to better serve your customers.

4. Be efficient. Don't make customers wait for reorders, unless you are trying to slow down their rate of drinking. Stay alert for accidental spills or special needs of guests. Find something to do, keep moving. When you work efficiently, the impression you give to

your customers, is that you are working hard for them. They like that and appreciate it. Be efficient but do not rush your customers. And in all instances, monitor your customers' drinking patterns carefully to prevent overindulging.

Appendix

C

STATE ALCOHOLIC BEVERAGE CONTROL BOARDS

Following is a list of the state agencies that administer and enforce the laws governing the production, distribution, and serving of alcoholic beverages:

ALABAMA
Alcoholic Beverage
Control Board
2715 Gunter Park Dr., W.
Montgomery, AL 36109
(205) 271-3840

ALASKA
Alcoholic Beverage Control Board
Dept. of Revenue
550 W. Seventh St., Ste. 350
Anchorage, AK 99501
(907) 277-8638

ARIZONA
Dept. of Liquor Licenses & Control
800 W. Washington, Ste. 500
Phoenix, AZ 85007
(602) 542-5141

ARKANSAS
Alcoholic Beverage Control
 Administration
100 Main St., Rm. 503
Little Rock, AR 72201
(501) 682-1105

CALIFORNIA
Dept. of Alcoholic Beverage Control
1901 Broadway
Sacramento, CA 95818
(916) 445-3221

COLORADO
Liquor Enforcement Div.
Dept. of Revenue
1375 Sherman St., Rm. 628
Denver, CO 80203
(303) 866-3741

CONNECTICUT
Liquor Control Comm.
Dept. of Liquor Control
165 Capitol Ave., Rm. 556
Hartford, CT 06106
(203) 566-4687

DELAWARE
Alcoholic Beverage Control Comm.
820 N. French St.
Wilmington, DE 19801
(302) 577-3200

FLORIDA
Alcoholic Beverages & Tobacco
Dept. of Business & Professional
 Regulation
725 S. Bronough St.
Tallahassee, FL 32399
(904) 488-7891

GEORGIA
Alcohol & Tobacco Tax Unit
Dept. of Revenue
270 Washington St., S.W.
Atlanta, GA 30334
(404) 656-4252

IDAHO
Alcohol Beverage Control Div.
Dept. of Law Enforcement
P.O. Box 55
Boise, ID 83707
(208) 334-3628

ILLINOIS
Liquor Control Comm.
100 W. Randolph, Ste. 5-300
Chicago, IL 60601
(312) 814-3930

INDIANA
Alcoholic Beverage Comm.
302 W. Washington St., Rm. E114
Indianapolis, IN 46204
(317) 232-2448

IOWA
Alcoholic Beverage Div.
Dept. of Commerce
1918 S.E. Hulsizer
Ankeny, IA 50021
(515) 281-7401

KANSAS
Alcoholic Beverage Control Div.
Dept. of Revenue
4 Townsite Plz., Ste. 210
120 E. Sixth
Topeka, KS 66603
(913) 296-3946

KENTUCKY
Alcoholic Beverage Control
123 Walnut St.
Frankfort, KY 40601
(502) 564-4850

LOUISIANA
Off. of Alcoholic Beverage Control
Dept. of Public Safety & Corrections
P.O. Box 66404
Baton Rouge, LA 70896
(504) 925-4041

MAINE
Bur. of Alcoholic Beverages & Lottery
 Operations
State House Station # 8
Augusta, ME 04333
(207) 287-3721

MARYLAND
Alcohol & Tobacco Tax Div.
State Treasury Bldg., Rm. 310
Annapolis, MD 21401
(410) 974-3319

MASSACHUSETTS
Alcoholic Beverages Control Comm.
100 Cambridge St., Rm. 2204
Boston, MA 02202
(617) 727-3040

MICHIGAN
Liquor Control Comm.
Dept. of Commerce
7150 Harris Dr.
Lansing, MI 48909
(517) 322-1353

MINNESOTA
Liquor Control Div.
Dept. of Public Safety
190 5th St., E., Rm. 105
St. Paul, MN 55101
(612) 296-6159

MISSISSIPPI
Alcoholic Beverage Control Div.
State Tax Comm.
P.O. Box 540
Madison, MS 39130
(601) 359-1098

MISSOURI
Dept. of Liquor Control
Dept. of Public Safety
301 W. High St.
Jefferson City, MO 65102
(314) 751-2333

MONTANA
Liquor Div.
Dept. of Revenue
2517 Airport Rd.
Helena, MT 59624
(406) 444-0700

NEBRASKA
Liquor Control Comm.
301 Centennial Mall S.
P.O. Box 95046
Lincoln, NE 68509
(402) 471-2571

NEW HAMPSHIRE
Liquor Comm.
P.O. Box 503
Concord, NH 03302
(603) 271-3132

NEW JERSEY
Alcoholic Beverage Control Div.
Dept. of Law & Public Safety
TRW Complex, CN087
Trenton, NJ 08265
(609) 984-3230

NEW MEXICO
Alcohol & Gaming Div.
Dept. of Regulation & Licensing
725 St. Michaels Dr.
Santa Fe, NM 87501
(505) 827-7066

NEW YORK
State Liquor Authority
250 Broadway
New York, NY 10007
(212) 417-4191

NORTH CAROLINA
Alcohol Beverage Control Comm.
Dept. of Commerce
3322 Old Garner Rd.
Raleigh, NC 27610
(919) 779-0700

NORTH DAKOTA
Off. of Attorney General
State Capitol, 17th Fl.
600 E. Boulevard Ave.
Bismarck, ND 58505
(701) 224-2210

OHIO
Dept. of Liquor Control
2323 W. Fifth Ave.
Columbus, OH 43226
(614) 644-2472

OKLAHOMA
Alcoholic Beverage Control Board
2501 N. Stiles
Oklahoma City, OK 73105
(405) 521-3484

OREGON
Liquor Control
9079 S.E. McLoughlin Blvd.
Portland, OR 97222
(503) 653-3018

PENNSYLVANIA
Liquor Control Board
532 Northwest Off. Bldg.
Harrisburg, PA 17124
(717) 787-2696

RHODE ISLAND
Liquor Control
Dept. of Business Regulation
233 Richmond St.
Providence, RI 02903
(401) 277-2562

SOUTH CAROLINA
Dept. of Revenue & Taxation
Div. of Alcohol Beverage Control &
  Licensing
301 Gervais St.
Columbia, SC 29201
(803) 734-0477

SOUTH DAKOTA
Div. of Special Taxes
Dept. of Revenue
Kneip Bldg., 3rd Fl.
Pierre, SD 57501
(605) 773-3311

TENNESSEE
Alcoholic Beverage Comm.
226 Capitol Blvd., Ste. 300
Nashville, TN 37243
(615) 741-1602

TEXAS
Alcoholic Beverage Comm.
P.O. Box 13127, Capitol Station
Austin, TX 78711
(512) 458-2500

UTAH
Liquor Control Comm.
1625 S. 900 W.
P.O. Box 30408
Salt Lake City, UT 84130
(801) 973-7770

VERMONT
Dept. of Liquor Control
Green Mountain Dr.
Montpelier, VT 05602
(802) 828-2345

VIRGINIA
Dept. of Alcoholic Beverage Control
2901 Hermitage Rd.
Richmond, VA 23220
(804) 367-0627

WASHINGTON
Liquor Control Board
1025 E. Union St.
P.O. Box 43705
Olympia, WA 98504
(206) 753-6262

WEST VIRGINIA
Alcoholic Beverage Control
310 57th St., S.E.
Charleston, WV 25305
(304) 558-2481

WISCONSIN
Alcohol & Tobacco Enforcement
Dept. of Revenue
P.O. Box 8905
Madison, WI 53708
(608) 266-6701

WYOMING
Liquor Comm.
1520 E. Fifth St.
Cheyenne, WY 82002
(307) 777-6453

DISTRICT OF COLUMBIA
Alcoholic Beverage
Control Div.
Dept. of Consumer & Regulatory Affairs
614 H St., N.W., Rm. 807
Washington, DC 20001
(202) 727-7377

PUERTO RICO
Bur. of Alcoholic Beverage Taxes
Dept. of Treasury
P.O. Box S-4515
San Juan, PR 00905
(809) 721-2020

U.S. VIRGIN ISLANDS
Dept. of Licensing & Consumer Affairs,
    Property & Procurement
Sub Base, Bldg. 1, Rm. 205
St. Thomas, VI 00802
(809) 774-3130

Source: State Administrative Officials
Classified by Function 1993-94, published by the Council of State Governors

Appendix
D

STATE HEALTH DEPARTMENTS

Following is a list of state agencies that enforce public health laws in the state:

ALABAMA
Dept. of Public Health
434 Monroe St., Rm. 331
Montgomery, AL 36130
(205) 242-5052

ALASKA
Div. of Public Health
Dept. of Health & Social Services
P.O. Box 110610
Juneau, AK 99811
(907) 465-3090

ARIZONA
Dept. of Health Services
1740 W. Adams St.
Phoenix, AZ 85007
(602) 542-1025

ARKANSAS
Dept. of Health
4815 W. Markham St.
Little Rock, AR 72205
(501) 661-2417

CALIFORNIA
Dept. of Health Services
714 P St., Rm. 1253
Sacramento, CA 95814
(916) 657-1425

COLORADO
Dept. of Health
4300 Cherry Creek Dr., S.
Denver, CO 80222
(303) 692-2000

CONNECTICUT
Dept. of Health Services
150 Washington St.
Hartford, CT 06106
(203) 566-2038

DELAWARE
Div. of Public Health
Dept. of Health & Social Services
P.O. Box 637
Dover, DE 19903
(302) 739-4701

FLORIDA
Health Program Off.
Dept. of Health & Rehabilitative
  Services
1317 Winewood Blvd.
Tallahassee, FL 32399
(904) 487-2705

GEORGIA
Public Health Div.
Dept. of Human Div.
Dept. of Human Resources
2 Peachtree St., 7th Fl.
Atlanta, GA 30303
(404) 657-2702

HAWAII
Dept. of Health
P.O. Box 3378
Honolulu, HI 96801
(808) 586-4410

IDAHO
Dept. of Health & Welfare
450 W. State Towers, 10th Fl.
Boise, ID 83720
(208) 334-5500

ILLINOIS
Dept. of Public Health
535 W. Jefferson St.
Springfield, IL 62761
(217) 782-4977

INDIANA
State Board of Health
1330 W. Michigan St., # 4255
Indianapolis, IN 46206
(317) 633-8400

IOWA
Dept. of Public Health
Lucas State Off. Bldg.
Des Moines, IA 50319
(515) 281-5605

KANSAS
Dept. of Health & Environment
900 S.W. Jackson, Ste. 620
Topeka, KS 66612
(913) 296-1343

KENTUCKY
Dept. for Health Services
Cabinet for Human Resources
275 E. Main St.
Frankfort, KY 40601
(502) 564-3970

LOUISIANA
Dept. of Health & Hospitals
P.O. Box 3214
New Orleans, LA 70821
(504) 342-8092

MAINE
Dept. of Human Services
State House Station #11
Augusta, ME 04333
(207) 287-2736

MARYLAND
Dept. of Health & Mental Hygiene
201 W. Preston St., 5th Fl.
Baltimore, MD 21201
(410) 225-6500

MASSACHUSETTS
Dept. of Public Health
150 Tremont St.
Boston, MA 02111
(617) 727-0201

MICHIGAN
Dept. of Public Health
3500 N. Logan
P.O. Box 30035
Lansing, MI 48909
(517) 335-8024

MINNESOTA
Dept. of Health
717 Delaware St., S.E.
P.O. Box 9441
Minneapolis, MN 55440
(612) 623-5460

MISSOURI
Dept. of Health
P.O. Box 570
Jefferson City, MO 65102
(314) 751-6001

MONTANA
Health Services Div.
Dept. of Health & Environmental
    Sciences
Cogswell Bldg.
Helena, MT 59620
(406) 444-4473

NEBRASKA
Dept. of Health
P.O. Box 95007
Lincoln, NE 68509
(402) 471-2133

NEVADA
Health Div.
Dept. of Human Resources
505 E. King St., Rm. 201
Carson City, NV 89710
(702) 687-4740

NEW HAMPSHIRE
Div. of Public Health Services
Dept. of Health & Human Services
Annex Bldg. 1
115 Pleasant St.
Concord, NH 03301
(603) 271-4505

NEW JERSEY
Dept. of Health
John Fitch Plz., CN360
Trenton, NJ 08625
(609) 292-4010

NEW MEXICO
Dept. of Health
1190 St. Frasncis Dr.
Santa Fe, NM 87502
(505) 827-2613

NEW YORK
Dept. of Health
Corning Tower
Empire State Plz.
Albany, NY 12237
(518) 474-2011

NORTH CAROLINA
Div. of Health Services
Dept. of Environment, Health &
    Natural Resources
P.O. Box 27687
Raleigh, NC 27611
(919) 733-7081

NORTH DAKOTA
Dept. of Health
600 E. Boulevard Ave.
Bismarck, ND 58505
(701) 224-2372

OHIO
Dept. of Health
246 N. High St.
P.O. Box 118
Columbus, OH 43266
(614) 466-2253

OKLAHOMA
Dept. of Health
1000 N.E. 10th
P.O. Box 53551
Oklahoma City, OK 73152
(405) 271-4200

OREGON
Health Div.
Dept. of Human Resources
800 N.E. Oregon St., # 21
Portland, OR 97232
(503)229-5032

PENNSYLVANIA
Dept. of Health
802 Health & Welfare Bldg.
Harrisburg, PA 17120
(717) 787-6436

RHODE ISLAND
Dept. of Health
3 Capitol Hill
Providence, RI 02908
(401) 277-2231

SOUTH CAROLINA
Health & Environmental Control
2600 Bull St.
Columbia, SC 29201
(803) 734-4880

SOUTH DAKOTA
Dept. of Health
445 E. Capitol Ave.
Pierre, SD 57501
(605) 773-3361

TENNESSEE
Dept. of Health
344 Cordell Hull Bldg.
Nashville, TN 37427
(615) 741-3111

TEXAS
Dept. of Health
1100 W. 49th St.
Austin, TX 78756
(512) 458-7111

UTAH
Dept. of Health
288 N. 1460 W.
Salt Lake, City, UT 84116
(801) 538-6111
also:
Government & Community Relations
288 N. 1460 W.
P.O. Box 16700
Salt Lake City, UT 84116
(801) 538-6332

VERMONT
Dept. of Health
108 Cherry St.
P.O. Box 70
Burlington, VT 05402
(802) 863-7280

VIRGINIA
Dept. of Health
400 James Madison Bldg.
109 Governor St.
Richmond, VA 23219
(804) 786-3561

WASHINGTON
Dept. of Health
P.O. Box 47890
Olympia, WA 98504
(206) 586-5846

WEST VIRGINIA
Dept. of Health & Human Resources
Bldg. 3, Rm. 206
State Capitol Complex
Charleston, WV 25305
(304) 558-0684

Also:
Bur. of Public Health
Bldg.3 Rm. 519
1900 Kanawha Blvd., E.
Charleston, WV 23505
(304) 558-2971

WISCONSIN
Div. of Health
Dept. of Health & Social Services
1 W. Wilson St.
Madison, WI 53703
(608) 266-1511

WYOMING
Dept. of Health
Hathaway Bldg.
Cheyenne, WY 82002
(307) 777-7656

DISTRICT OF COLUMBIA
Comm. on Public Health
Dept. of Human Services
1660 L St., N.W., 12th Fl.
Washington, DC 20036
(202) 673-7700

PUERTO RICO
Dept. of Health
P.O. Box 70184
San Juan, PR 00936
(809) 250-7227

U.S. VIRGIN ISLANDS
Dept. of Health
St. Thomas Hospital
St. Thomas, VI 00802
(809) 776-8311

Source: State Administrative Officials
Classified by Function 1993-94, published by the Council of State Governors

Appendix
E

STATE HOSPITALITY ASSOCIATIONS

Following is a list of restaurant and hospitality associations, by state. Membership in these organizations provides an opportunity to meet and network with people in the bar and restaurant business who share similar concerns. The associations also provide educational programs.

Alabama Restaurant Assoc.
2100 Data
Suite 207
Birmingham, AL 36104
(205) 263-3407

Alaska Hotel & Motel Assoc.
P.O. Box 104900
Anchorage, AK 99510
(907) 563-7977

Arkansas Hospitality Assoc.
603 Pulaski St.
P.O. Box1556
Little Rock, AR 72203
(501) 376-2323

Arizona Restaurant Assoc.
2701 N. 16th St.
#221
Phoenix, AZ 85006

California Restaurant Assoc.
3435 Wilshire Blvd.
Suite 2606
Los Angeles, CA 90010
(213) 384-1200

Colorado Hotel & Motel Assoc.
999 18th St.
Suite 1240
Denver, CO 80202
(303) 592-1818

Connecticut Restaurant Assoc.
19 Wallingford Rd.
Chesire, CT 06410

Delaware Restaurant Assoc.
325 E. Main St.
Suite 300
Newark, DE 19714-6605

Georgia Hospitality & Travel Assoc.
600 W. Peachtree St.
Suite 1500
Atlanta, GA 30308
(404) 577-5888

Hawaii Restaurant Assoc.
1188 Bishop St.
Suite 2611
Honolulu 96813

Idaho Restaurant & Beverage Assoc.
P.O. Box 1638
Boise, ID 83701
  or:
Idaho Innkeepers Assoc.
P.O. Box 8212
Boise, ID 83707
(208) 362-2637

Illinois Restaurant Assoc.
350 W. Ontario
Chicago, IL 60610

Indiana Restaurant Assoc.
2120 N. Meridian St.
Indianapolis, IN 46202

Iowa Restaurant & Beverage Assoc.
606 Merele Hay Tower
Des Moines, IA 50310

Hotel/Motel Assoc. of Kansas
Suite 404 Midland Bldg.
1221 Baltimore Ave.
Kansas City, KS 64105
(816) 421-2072
  or:
Kansas Restaurant Assoc.
422 Executive Park
Louisville, KS 40207

Louisiana Restaurant Assoc.
2800 Veterans Blvd.
Suite 160
Metairie, LA 70002

Maine Restaurant Assoc.
5 Wade St.
P.O. Box 5060
Augusta, ME 04330-0552

Restaurant Assoc. of Maryland, Inc.
7113 Ambassador Rd.
Baltimore, MD 21207

Massachusetts Restaurant Assoc.
95-A Turnpike
Westborough, MA 01581-9775
(508) 366-4144
  or:
Massachusetts Hotel-Motel Assoc.
148 State St.
Suite 400
Boston, MA 02109-2508
(617) 720-1776

Michigan Restaurant Assoc.
200 N. Washington Sq.
Suite 10
Lansing, MI 48933
(517) 484-2444

Minnesota Restaurant Assoc. & Resort
  Assoc.
871 Jefferson Ave.
St. Paul, MN 55102

Mississippi Restaurant Assoc.
P.O. Box 16395
4506 Office Park Dr.
Jackson, MS 39236

Missouri Restaurant Assoc.
P.O. Box 10277
Kansas City, MO 64111
(816) 753-5222

Montana Restaurant Assoc.
P.O. Box 7998
Missoula, MT 59807

Nebraska Restaurant Assoc.
5625 o St. Bldg.
Suite 7
Lincoln, NE 68510

Nevada Restaurant Assoc.
4820 Alpine Placen
Suite B202
Las Vagas, NV 89107

New Jersey Restaurant Assoc.
853 Kearny Ave.
Kearny, NJ 07032

New Mexico Restaurant Assoc.
2140 San Mateo Blvd., N.E.
Suite C
Albuquerque, NM 87110
(505) 268-2474

North Dakota Hospitality Assoc.
P.O. Box 428
Bismark, ND 58502
(701) 223-3313

New York Restaurant Assoc.
505 8th Ave.
7th Fl.
New York, NY 10018

Ohio Restaurant Assoc.
1315 Dublin Rd.
Suite 208 D
Columbus, OH 43215

Oklahoma Restaurant Assoc.
380 N. Portland
Oklahoma City, OK 73112

Oregon Restaurant & Hospitality Assoc.
3724 N.E. Broadway
Portland, OR 97232
(503) 249-0974

Pennsylvania Restaurant Assoc.
501 N. Front St.
Suite 200
Harrisburg, PA 17101-1011

Rhode Island Hospitality Assoc.
P.O. Box 6208
Providence, RI 02942
(401) 334-3180

South Carolina Restaurant Assoc.
Barringer Bldg.
Suite 510
Columbia, SC 29201

South Dakota Restaurant Assoc.
P.O. Box 1173
Pierre, SD 57501

Tennessee Restaurant Assoc.
229 Court Sq.
P.O. Box 1029
Franklin, TN 37065

Texas Restaurant Assoc.
1400 Lavaca
Austin, TX 78701
(515) 472-3666

Utah Restaurant Assoc.
141 Haven Ave.
Suite 2
Salt Lake City, UT 84115

Vermont Lodging & Restaurant Assoc.
97 State St.
P.O. Box 9
Montpelier, VT 05602
(802) 229-0062

Virginia Restaurant Assoc.
2101 Libbie Ave.
Richmond, VA 23230

Restaurant Assoc. of Washington State
722 Securities Bldg.
Seattle, WA 98101
        or:
Restaurant Assoc. of Met. Washington
7926 Jones Branch Dr.
Suite 530
McLean, WA 22101-3390
(703) 356-1315

Hotel Assoc. of Washington, D.C.
1201 New York Ave, N.W.
Washington, DC 20005
(202) 833-3350

West Virginia Restaurant Assoc.
P.O. Box 2391
Charlestown, WV 25328

Wisconsin Restaurant Assoc.
125 Doty St.
Suite 200
Madison, WI 53703

Wyoming Lodging & Restaurant Assoc.
1723 Thomes Suite B
P.O. Box 1003
Cheyenne, WY 82003
(307) 634-8816

STATE LABOR DEPARTMENTS

Following is a list of state agencies that are responsible for administering and enforcing the state's labor laws:

ALABAMA
Dept. of Labor
1789 Congressman
Dickinson Dr., 2nd Fl.
Montgomery, AL 36130
(205) 242-3460

ALASKA
Dept. of Labor
P.O. Box 21149
Juneau, AK 99802
(907) 465-2700

ARIZONA
Industrial Comm.
P.O. Box 19070
Phoenix, AZ 85005
(602) 542-4411

ARKANSAS
Dept. of Labor
10421 W. Markham, Ste. 100
Little Rock, AZ 72205
(501) 682-4500

CALIFORNIA
Dept. of Industrial Relations
455 Golden Gate Ave.
San Francisco, CA 94102
(415) 703-4590

COLORADO
Dept. of Labor & Employment
1120 Lincoln St., 13th Fl.
Denver, CO 80203
(303) 894-7530

CONNECTICUT
Dept. of Labor
200 Folly Brook Blvd.
Wethersfield, CT 06109
(203) 566-4384

DELAWARE
Dept. of Labor
820 N. French St., 6th Fl.
Wilmington, DE 19801
(302) 577-2710

FLORIDA
Public Employee Relations Comm.
Turner Bldg.
Koger Executive Ctr.
Tallahassee, FL 32399
(904) 488-8641

GEORGIA
Dept. of Labor
148 International Blvd.
Atlanta, GA 30303
(404) 656-3011

HAWAII
Dept. of Labor & Industrial Relations
830 Punchbowl St.
Honolulu, HI 96813
(808) 586-8844

IDAHO
Labor & Industrial Services
277 N. Sixth St.
Boise, ID 83720
(208) 334-3950

ILLINOIS
Dept. of Labor
160 N. LaSalle St., Ste. C1300
Chicago, IL 60601
(312) 793-2800

INDIANA
Dept. of Labor
IGC-South, Rm. W195
402 W. Washington
Indianapolis, IN 46204
(317) 232-2663

IOWA
Div. of Labor Services
Dept. of Employment Services
1000 E. Grand
Des Moines, IA 50319
(515) 281-8067

KANSAS
Labor Management Relations &
    Employment Standards
Dept. of Human Resources
512 W. Sixth
Topeka, KS 66603
(913) 296-7475

KENTUCKY
Labor Cabinet
1049 U.S. 127 S.
Frankfort, KY 40601
(502) 564-3070

LOUISIANA
Dept. of Labor
P.O. Box 94094
Baton Rouge, LA 70804
(504) 342-3011

MAINE
Dept. of Labor
State House Station # 54
Augusta, ME 04333
(207) 287-3788

MARYLAND
Div. of Labor & Industry
Dept. of Licensing & Regulation
501 St. Paul Pl.
Baltimore, MD 21202
(410) 333-4179

MASSACHUSETTS
Dept. of Labor & Industries
Executive Off. of Labor
100 Cambridge St.
Boston, MA 02202
(617) 727-3454

MICHIGAN
Employment Security Comm.
Dept. of Labor
P.O. Box 30015
Lansing, MI 48909
(517) 373-9600

MINNESOTA
Dept. of Labor & Industry
443 Lafayette Rd.
St. Paul, MN 55101
(612) 296-2342

MISSOURI
Dept. of Labor & Industrial Relations
P.O. Box 504
Jefferson City, MO 65104
(314) 751-4091

MONTANA
Dept. of Labor & Industry
P.O. Box 1728
Helena, MT 59624
(406) 444-3555

NEBRASKA
Dept. of Labor
P.O. Box 94600
Lincoln, NE 68509
(402) 471-9000

NEVADA
Labor Comm.
1445 Hot Springs Rd., Ste. 108
Carson City, NV 89710
(702) 687-4850

NEW HAMPSHIRE
Dept. of Labor
95 Pleasant St.
Concord, NH 03301
(603) 271-3171

NEW JERSEY
Dept. of Labor
John Fitch Plz., CN110
Trenton, NJ 08625
(609) 292-2323

NEW MEXICO
Dept. of Labor
P.O. Box 1928
Albuquerque, NM 87103
(505) 841-8409

NEW YORK
Dept. of Labor
State Off. Bldg., State Campus
Albany, NY 12240
(518) 457-2741

NORTH CAROLINA
Dept. of Labor
4 W. Edenton St.
Raleigh, NC 27601
(919) 733-7166

NORTH DAKOTA
Dept. of Labor
State Capitol, 6th Fl.
600 E. Boulevard Ave.
Bismarck, ND 58505
(701) 224-2660

OHIO
Dept. of Industrial Relations
2333 W. Fifth Ave.
P.O. Box 825
Columbus, OH 43266
(614) 644-2223

OKLAHOMA
Dept. of Labor
1315 Broadway Pl.
Oklahoma City, OK 73103
(405) 521-2461

OREGON
Bur. of Labor & Industries
800 N.E. Oregon St.
Portland, OR 97232
(503) 229-5737

PENNSYLVANIA
Dept. of Labor & Industry
Labor & Industry Bldg., Rm. 1700
Harrisburg, PA 17120
(717) 787-2756

RHODE ISLAND
Dept. of Labor
220 Elmwood Ave.
Providence, RI 02907
(401) 457-1808

SOUTH CAROLINA
Dept. of Labor
P.O. Box 11329
Columbia, SC 29211
(803) 734-9600

SOUTH DAKOTA
Dept. of Labor
700 Governors Dr.
Pierre, SD 57501
(605) 773-3101

TENNESSEE
Dept. of Labor
501 Union St.
Nashville, TN 37243
(615) 741-2582

TEXAS
Dept. of Labor Laws
Employment Comm.
3520 Executive Ctr. Dr., # 320
Austin, TX 78731
(515) 463-2222

UTAH
State Industrial Comm.
160 E. 300S
Salt Lake City, UT 84111
(801) 530-6800

VERMONT
Dept. of Labor & Industry
National Life Buldg.
P.O. Drawer 20
Montpelier, VT 05620
(802) 828-2286

VIRGINIA
Dept. of Labor & Industry
13 S. 13th St.
Richmond, VA 23219
(804) 786-2377

WASHINGTON
Dept. of Labor & Industries
P.O. Box 44001
Olympia, WA 98504
(206) 956-4202

WEST VIRGINIA
Div. of Labor
State Capitol Complex, Bldg. 3
Charleston, WV 25305
(304) 558-7890

WISCONSIN
Dept. of Industrial Labor & Human
    Relations
201 E. Washington Ave.
P.O. Box 7946
Madison, WI 53707
(608) 266-7552

WYOMING
Div. of Labor Standards
Dept. of Employment
Herschler Bldg.
Cheyenne, WY 82002
(307) 777-7435

DISTRICT OF COLUMBIA
Dept. of Employment Services
500 C St., N.W., Rm. 600
Washington, DC 20001
(202) 724-7101

GUAM
Dept. of Labor
P.O. Box 9970
Tamuning, GU 96911
(671) 646-9241

NORTHERN MARIANA ISLANDS
Dept. of Commerce & Labor
Off. of the Governor
Saipan, MP 96950
(670) 322-4361

PUERTO RICO
Dept. of Labor & Human Resources
505 Munoz Rivera Ave.
Hato Rey, PR 00918
(809) 754-5353

U.S. VIRGIN ISLANDS
Dept. of Labor
P.O. Box 890
Christiansted
St. Croix, VI 00820
(809) 773-1994

Source: State Administrative Officials
Classified by Function 1993-94, pub-
lished by the Council of State
Governors.

RESOURCES FOR SMALL BUSINESS

Upstart Publishing Company, Inc. The following publications on proven management techniques for small businesses are available from Upstart Publishing Company, Inc., 12 Portland St., Dover, NH 03820. For a free current catalog, call (800) 235-8866 outside New Hampshire, or 749-5071 in state.

The Business Planning Guide, 6th edition, 1992, David H. Bangs, Jr. and Upstart Publishing Company, Inc. A manual that helps you write a business plan and financing proposal tailored to your business, your goals, and your resources. Includes worksheets and checklists. (Softcover, 208 pp., $19.95)

The Market Planning Guide, 4th edition, 1994, David H. Bangs, Jr. and Upstart Publishing Company, Inc. A manual to help small-business owners put together a goal-oriented, resource-based marketing plan with action steps, benchmarks, and time lines. Includes worksheets and checklists to make implementation and review easier. (Softcover, 180 pp., $19.95)

The Cash Flow Control Guide, 1990, David H. Bangs, Jr. and Upstart Publishing Company, Inc. A manual to help small-business owners solve their number one financial problem. Includes worksheets and checklists. (Softcover, 88 pp., $14.95)

The Personnel Planning Guide, 1988, David H. Bangs, Jr. and Upstart Publishing Company, Inc. A 176-page manual outlining practical, proven personnel management techniques, including hiring, managing, evaluating and compensating personnel. Includes worksheets and checklists. (Softcover, 176 pp., $19.95)

The Start Up Guide: A One-Year Plan for Entrepreneurs, 2nd edition, 1994, David H. Bangs, Jr. and Upstart Publishing Company, Inc. This book utilizes the same step-by-step, no-jargon method as *The Business Planning Guide*, to help even those with no business training through the process of beginning a successful business. (Softcover, 176 pp., $19.95)

Managing By the Numbers: Financial Essentials for the Growing Business, 1992, David H. Bangs, Jr. and Upstart Publishing Company, Inc. Straightforward techniques for getting the maximum return with a minimum of detail in your business's financial management. (Softcover, 160 pp., $19.95)

Building Wealth, 1992, David H. Bangs, Jr. and the editors of *Common Sense*. A collection of tested techniques designed to help you plan your personal finances and how to plan your business finances to benefit you, your family, and employees. (Softcover, 168 pp., $19.95)

Buy the Right Business—At the Right Price, 1990, Brian Knight and the Associates of Country Business, Inc. Many people who would like to be in business for themselves think strictly of starting a business. In some cases, buying a going concern may be preferable—and just as affordable. (Softcover, 152 pp., $18.95)

Borrowing for Your Business, 1991, George M. Dawson. This is a book for borrowers and about lenders. Includes detailed guidelines on how to select a bank and a banker, how to answer the lender's seven most important questions, how your banker looks at a loan, and how to get a loan renewed. (Hardcover, 160 pp., $19.95)

Can This Partnership Be Saved?, 1992, Peter Wylie and Mardy Grothe. The authors offer solutions and hope for problems between key people in business. (Softcover, 272 pp., $19.95)

The Complete Guide to Selling Your Business, 1992, Paul Sperry and Beatrice Mitchell. A step-by-step guide through the entire process from how to determine when the time is right to sell to negotiating the final terms. (Hardcover, 160 pp., $21.95)

The Complete Selling System, 1991, Pete Frye. This book can help any manager or salesperson, even those with no experience, find the solutions to some of the most common dilemmas in managing sales. (Hardcover, 192 pp., $21.95)

Creating Customers, 1992, David H. Bangs, Jr. and the editors of *Common Sense*. A book for business owners and managers who want a step-by-step approach to selling and promoting. Techniques include inexpensive market research, pricing your goods and services, and writing a usable marketing plan. (Softcover, 176 pp., $19.95)

The Entrepreneur's Guide to Going Public, 1994, James B. Arkebauer with Ron Schultz. A comprehensive and useful book on a subject that is the ultimate dream of most entrepreneurs—making an initial public offering IPO). (Softcover, 368 pp., $19.95)

Financial Troubleshooting, 1992, David H. Bangs, Jr. and the editors of *Common Sense.* This book helps the owner/manager use basic diagnostic methods to monitor the health of the business and solve problems before damage occurs. (Softcover, 192 pp., $19.95)

Financial Essentials for Small Business Success, 1994, Joseph Tabet and Jeffrey Slater. Designed to show readers where to get the information they need and how planning and recordkeeping will enhance the health of any small business. (Softcover, 272 pp., $19.95)

Keeping the Books, 1993, Linda Pinson and Jerry Jinnett. Basic business recordkeeping both explained and illustrated. Designed to give you a clear understanding of small business accounting by taking you step-by-step through general records, development of financial statements, tax reporting, scheduling, and financial statement analysis. (Softcover, 208 pp., $19.95)

The Language of Small Business, 1994, Carl O. Trautmann. A clear, concise dictionary of small business terms for students and small business owners. (Softcover, 416 pp., $19.95)

Steps to Small Business Start-Up, 1993, Linda Pinson and Jerry Jinnett. A step-by-step guide for starting and succeeding with a small or home-based business. Takes you through the mechanics of business start-up and gives an overview of information on such topics as copyrights, trademarks, legal structures, recordkeeping, and marketing. (Softcover, 256 pp., $19.95)

Target Marketing for the Small Business, 1993, Linda Pinson and Jerry Jinnett. A comprehensive guide to marketing your business. This book not only shows you how to reach your customers, it also gives you a wealth of information on how to research that market through the use of library resources, questionnaires, demographics, etc. (Softcover, 176 pp., $19.95)

On Your Own: A Woman's Guide to Starting Your Own Business, 2nd edition, 1993, Laurie Zuckerman. *On Your Own* is for women who want hands-on, practical information about starting and running their own business. It deals honestly with issues like finding time for your business when you're also the primary care provider, societal biases against women ,and credit discrimination. (Softcover, 320 pp., $19.95)

Problem Employees, 1991, Dr. Peter Wylie and Dr. Mardy Grothe. Provides managers and supervisors with a simple, practical, and straight-forward approach to help all employees, especially problem employees, significantly improve their work performance. (Softcover, 272 pp., $22.95)

Problems and Solutions in Small Business Management, 1994, The editors of *Forum*, the journal of the Association of Small Business Development Centers. A collection of case studies selected from the pages of *Forum* magazine. (Softcover, 200 pp., $21.95)

The Restaurant Planning Guide, 1992, Peter Rainsford and David H. Bangs, Jr. This book takes the practical techniques of *The Business Planning Guide* and combines them with the expertise of Peter Rainsford, a professor at the Cornell School of Hotel Administration and restaura-teur. Topics include: establishing menu prices, staffing and scheduling, controlling costs and niche marketing. (Softcover, 176 pp., $19.95)

Successful Retailing, 2nd edition, 1993, Paula Wardell. Provides hands-on help for those who want to start or expand their retail business. Sections include: strategic planning, marketing and market research, and invento-ry control. (Softcover, 176 pp., $19.95)

The Woman Entrepreneur, 1992, Linda Pinson and Jerry Jinnett. Thirty-three successful women business owners share their practical ideas for suc-cess and their sources for inspiration. (Softcover, 244 pp., $14.00)

Other Available Titles

The Complete Guide to Business Agreements, 1993, Ted Nicholas, Enterprise • Dearborn. Contains 127 of the most commonly needed busi-ness agreements. (Loose-leaf binder, $69.95)

The Complete Small Business Legal Guide, 1993, Robert Friedman, Enterprise • Dearborn. Provides the hands-on help you need to start a business, maintain all necessary records, properly hire and fire employees ,and deal with the many changes a business goes through. (Softcover, $69.95)

Forecasting Sales and Planning Profits: A No-Nonsense Guide for Growing a Business, 1986, Kenneth E. Marino, Probus Publishing Co. Concise and easily applied forecasting system based on an analysis of market potential and sales requirements, which helps establish the basis for financial statements in your business plan. Book is currently out of print, check second-hand bookstores for the title.

Guerrilla Marketing: Secrets for Making Big Profits from Your Small Business, 1984, J. Conrad Levinson, Houghton-Mifflin. A classic tool kit for small businesses. (Hardcover, 226 pp., $14.95)

Marketing Sourcebook for Small Business, 1989, Jeffrey P. Davidson, John Wylie Publishing. A good introductory book for small business owners with excellent definitions of important marketing terms and concepts. (Hardcover, 325 pp., $24.95)

The Small Business Survival Kit: 101 Troubleshooting Tips for Success, 1993, John Ventura, Enterprise • Dearborn. Offers compassionate insight into the emotional side of financial difficulties as well as a nuts and bolts consideration of options for the small businessperson experiencing tough times. (Softcover, $19.95)

INDEX